# HOW TO GROW
# MSMEs
# FAST?

## A Basic Initial Guide For
## MSMEs & STARTUPs

I0480018

## THAMIZHAZHAGAN
## NALLAIYAN

INDIA · SINGAPORE · MALAYSIA

## Notion Press

Old No. 38, New No. 6
McNichols Road, Chetpet
Chennai - 600 031

First Published by Notion Press 2020
Copyright © Thamizhazhagan Nallaiyan 2020
All Rights Reserved.

ISBN 978-1-64899-627-6

DEDICATED TO MY PARENTS

# Contents

# Introduction

When we say DO BUSINESS! DO BUSINESS! Most people think of struggles and fears. The basic reasons for this are fear of failure and insecure mindset. Further it is ignorance of various industrial help programs, offers, and the business consultancy and help centers. This book resolves that ignorance and the fears.

For those hesitant to do business due to the above reasons, in order to clearly understand all of the business help programs of the government of India, and their offers, this book of Mr. Thamizhazhagan Nallaiyan shall render great benefits. Though there may be many programs, this book tells you when to use the apropos program.

**Further people should be "Job givers rather than Job seekers"** based on which, joy, pride and satisfaction is obtained for having offered an employment to many people. **Mr. Thamizhazhagan Nallaiyan knows about this Formula** and has realized that with this formula more and more MSMEs can be created in our country, and has written this book excellently.

**Mr. Thamizhazhagan Nallaiyan who** has counselled many entrepreneurs and guided them, has offered the various schemes in simple words which are well understood and beneficial due to which this book will be very useful in guiding aspiring and existing entrepreneurs and to make them succeed in their business.

The schemes that are initiated via the **District Industrial Center, the National Small Industries Organization, MSME-DIs,** have been selected carefully and those that are immediately required by the **MSMEs** and **Startups**, and those that are required during initial stage have been listed in order.

Via the business knowledge and experience gathered over years, have been written by **Mr. Thamizhazhagan Nallaiyan,** and put forth in this book, there is no doubt that aspiring and existing entrepreneurs would read this and obtain success.

**– Mr. G.P. Lenin**
Engineer (1969), Entrepreneur
Mentor – Stand-up India Scheme
Member – Affirmative Action Committee of CII

 I take great pleasure in writing the preface of this book **HOW TO GROW FAST MSMEs?** written by **Mr. Thamizhazhagan Nallaiyan.** I have collaborated with him for the past eight years, having participated in various government and private programs concerning the MSMEs, I have witnessed the way he has worked and his process of action based in which I am writing preface.

I am well familiar with **Mr. Thamizhazhagan Nallaiyan, who has written** this book **HOW TO GROW FAST MSMEs?** From the year 2012. He is in touch with various MSMEs. I am aware that he is the key participant in framing nice policies which would be helpful for MSMEs in coordination with the government.

This book has been divided in to 10 parts starting with What are MSMEs? The difficulties in running them? How to access the solution to these problems? How to market their products? What are the government opportunities for them? What are the financial supports for continual operations of these enterprises? What are the organizations and institutions helping to the MSMEs continuously? What are the schemes and programs run based on these? Where are those offices and their addresses?

Hence the required information of each MSME, the procedures, have been written duly in a attractive way, and in a way that is simple and can be understood by all.

I believe that this book will be a great guideline for aspiring entrepreneurs and college students. I also believe that the existing entrepreneurs of the MSMEs will also benefit from the information in this book on how to grow their business.

I offer my heartfelt best wishes for the growth of this book which has been written for the first time in the literary efforts of Mr. Thamizhazhagan Nallaiyan, and his literary skills.

**– Mr. CK Mohan**
Entrepreneur
Former General Secretory of TANSTIA
EC Member of MSME Committee SICCI

# Preface

There are many troubles faced by the **MSMEs** which is considered the **"cradle of business entrepreneurship"** which supports the export business, which offers job opportunities to large people. But the risks faced by them are countless.

Though the MSMEs face many issues such as financial constrictions, licensing issues, the procedural difficulties in daily life, knowledge sharing and lack of guidelines are the main hindrance to their growth, also the lack of awareness of surrounding opportunities. The main reason for not availing these opportunities is the inbuilt psychological restrictions.

To overcome difficulties the main speed breakers are such mental barriers. I believe that this book will be a bridge to overcome your speed breakers and to grow your business fast.

Like a friend speaks to another friend, this book has been written to offer the action plans having realized the difficulties of the MSMEs. This book has been written offering a 360 degree view of the problems faced by the MSMEs.

I am offering you a feast of cocktail of fruit juices keeping in mind the difficulties faced by me as an MSME, the lessons learnt from them, the knowledge I obtained for relieving these issues like the time lapse, financial restrictions etc.

It has been created like a hand manual, which facilitates periodic review, wherein no requisite information is left out, based on the premise that there should be a detailed glimpse which is available as a briefing in a single book, so that there should not be a worry at a later stage that **"I was ignorant for so many years, I would have survived had I known of these at the earlier stage"**

The cost you would spent for this book is a capital investment. Hence if this book is used properly, we can attain a stage where a business can be started in any corner of India and business flags hoisted.

This book has been written such that chapters which was not viewed in an interconnected way is clubbed in a single place.

When you finish reading this book, you will get an awareness and a confidence that you can fill the entire Indian landscape with your business. For further doubts you can contact me via tamizhazhagan@ lemooria.org and resolve the same. I am always ready to help you.

Thanks and regards

**– Thamizhazhagan Nallaiyan**

Author

## Chapter 1

# What Are MSMEs?

## Definitions

Worldwide MSMEs are classified based on many definitions. The government takes initiatives in classifying the companies coming under MSMEs and offering guidelines that is because the MSMEs globally offer the maximum employment and substantial support to export business. When researching various nations, and when compared, each nation offers 6–98% of the employment based on the growth of the MSMEs. Each new entrepreneur and MSMEs should understand this situation, the government initiative, the society's necessities and the immediate needs.

## Industrial Types

The businesses are classified as **production, value addition, distribution, retail, aggregation**, and the **logistics** that connects all of them.

Each of the above businesses, are classified as per the activities. This way the global governments follow different parameters to help in their activities.

Further the seven types are classified in to three major group namely **manufacturing, service and trading.**

The small and micro medium enterprises are defined in many ways by the various nations. In some nations the employment opportunities of the MSMEs is used as a base for definition. Some others classify them based on the turnover. Some others use the capital investments for the classification.

Our country India too classifies the MSMEs based on the capital investments. The investment should be only meant for the instruments, machinery, and the factories built for them. Else the capital is not accounted for. These organization should be under the Manufacturing and service Industry. This is the procedure in our nation. This should be understood by all MSMEs. Without the government help the MSMEs cannot grow. We need to realize all of these.

## Types of Business

| S NO | TYPE | SERVICE | Manufacturing |
|------|------|---------|---------------|
| 1 | **MICRO** | TILL ₹ 10 LAKHS | TILL ₹ 25 LAKHS |
| 2 | **SMALL** | FROM ₹ 10 LAKHS TO ₹ 2 CRORES | FROM ₹ 25 LAKHS TO ₹ 5 CRORES |
| 3 | **MEDIUM** | FROM ₹ 2 CRORES TO ₹ 5CRORES | FROM ₹ 5 CRORES TO ₹ 10 CRORES |

## Micro Enterprises

In **Micro industries** relating to **service,** the investment for **equipment** of the enterprise should not exceed ₹ 10 Lakhs in case of **manufacturing** the investment for **factory** and **equipment** should not exceed ₹ 25 lakhs.

## Small Enterprises

In **small industries** relating to **service,** the Investment for **Machinery** of the enterprise should be between ₹ 10 Lakhs and ₹ 2 crores in case of **manufacturing** the Investment for **Plant and Machinery** should be between ₹ 25 lakhs and ₹ 5 crores.

## Medium Enterprises

In **medium industries** relating to **service,** the Investment for **Machinery** of the enterprise should be between ₹ 2 crores and ₹ 5 crores in case of **Manufacturing** the Investment for **Plant and Machinery** should be between ₹ 5 crores and ₹ 10 crores.

The definition of the above mentioned small, micro and medium enterprises is based on the government stance as of **May 2020**. They can change at a later date. It is of mention that there was a debate in the parliament that the total annual turnover should be the basis for the definition.

The subject that the new entrepreneur is ignorant of are the difference between **manufacturing, service and trade** industry. Hence under the title of definition I wish to clarify the details and definitions.

**Manufacturing** industry is producing a product using a raw material and certain services. There a product is created. But service doesn't produce any product. Rather it relates the service related a created product. The service can enhance the product value else it might not. The producer creates a product in lieu of money. The service industry provides a service in lieu of money. The tradesman gets a product from one person and sells it to another person.

**For example,** persons who make threads out of cotton, the fabric out of the thread, the cloth out of the fabric are all coming under **manufacturing industry**. For each person creates a new product. But persons who color the fabric, wash the fabric, and iron the fabric are coming under **service industry** and because they don't produce anything, only they adding service. The person who purchases and sells threads, the persons who purchase and sell fabrics and those who purchase and sell clothes are all coming under **trading industry**. For they don't produce any product nor offer any service. They merely get a product from one person and sells it to another person. But all of these are industries.

I believe that now you would have had a realization. I have clearly elucidated the business types, details of the small, micro and medium industries, Manufacturing, service, and their details etc.

Don't proceed to the next chapter without grasping this one. Read it several times and then proceed to the next.

Each person asks me about the choice of business, but if you walk through a shopping arcade each of it is a business. But in our nation the business is classified on the basis of caste. They are functioning as small groups. All members in the group are not into business. Most don't have the inclination to do business also. Others don't have the opportunity to conduct business. It's a curse to the nation's growth, because most of the businesses are locked down in such caste groups. It also stops the freedom of choosing business.

But after the Independence, opportunities become abound. The financial reforms that happened after 1990 around the world has created more opportunities. Globalization has created the opportunities for MNCs to come here and for our businesses to go to other countries. Under this situation the government has been focusing on the MSMEs. I have clarified earlier as to why the focus was on MSMEs.

Who are the persons who came to business later? Most of them are the first generation entrepreneurs. Some had created businesses with the help of some kind of family money or started business with a business background. But Most of them are the first generation entrepreneurs.

The ones running micro and small businesses are the ones that know that they won't get a government job in the age of 35–45 and not having sufficient experience, and they are under the restraint that they won't be getting a private job also with a good salary.

Some of them claim that it is a childhood passion for entrepreneurship like the various global entrepreneurs are very few. Since there is no job opportunities and not having money for running one's life, and since the government is helping to start a business, based on compulsion and based on the concept that it is an alternative way of earning, most of the small and micro industries are started. That means those all created for survival not as a passion.

But the current generation has a bit of change of mindset. Entrepreneurship has become the dream of a few. Start-ups has become the culture between the new generation people. But those enterprises also start off as a small and micro industries and disappear also as small and micro industries.

My opinion is that the reasons for the above is a lack of proper awareness. On one hand the government is struggling to grow the MSMEs with various schemes, on the other hand, those commencing a small industry, are struggling to grow their industry.

But the lack of coordination between these two (Government and MSMEs) leads to a major confusion. To clear the confusion between the MSMEs, the government has created various organizations. The difference between the number of registered entrepreneurs in that Government organizations, and the ones working in fields is like that of a mountain and a molehill.

The lack of awareness of the happenings in the business surroundings by the entrepreneurs is the reason for the business not growing. When the government is ready to help, not availing the same and not being aware of that is the main reason for failure. There are many reasons for failure and I will clarify that in the next chapter.

## Chapter 2

# Why Do MSMEs Fail?

Most of the MSMEs fail at the speed in which they commence. 99% of the start-ups fail. They close down within 3 years of their commencement. Do you feel that I am discussing failure at the onset? Don't think as to why you should think in the negative.

Left to me, there is no business failures. Each victory lends growth. Each failure teaches a lesson. Lessons prepare you for the next success. Those who don't learn from the failures are the ones that are failures as per me. Hence the victories give success and failures the preparation for the next success.

It is my opinion that one should learn from failures which is the first lesson in business. Don't think that I am being so philosophical. Though it looks like a philosophy it is the truth. So does it imply that we are starting a business to learn lessons? We are doing so to earn money. I wish to take out the term failure and change it to sliding. For slides are an aspect of a journey.

In our childhood we slide and fall down and learn to walk. After learning to walk we learn to run. We don't start running from the moment we are born. If we were to consider the child phase of sliding as failure, we will be unable to walk now. Those slides are the lessons by which we make a royal stride, to walk carefully and to run fast.

Ok. when do we attain our aims by merely sliding? When will my journey conclude? When will be victorious. When will I earn money? These are the various possible claims in your mind.

Without preparation you cannot succeed. As per my details I have mentioned earlier that preparation is learning from the failures and slides. In order to be prepared and to learn we cannot be chasing failures. But we can learn from others failures. Hence I have written on the various challenges faced by MSMEs, and the various reasons for failure and under the chapter, "why do MSMEs fail?".

## Challenges

### Lack of Core Field Knowledge

When wondering about the choice of business to start, the ones into MSMEs focus on the ones that others are already successful in. They think that by doing that business they too can succeed. Do you know which category of persons they consult for knowing about their business? They ask their brothers and the nearby persons. They consult their **friends**. They discuss it with their **relatives**. But none of them are entrepreneurs. Then if we act per their advice, will it be useful or not?

On feeling that they need to start a project report for any industry, most of them don't create a project report. They end up paying auditors to create a project report. When a business is created on the basis of such a plan by procuring a loan if possible, it ends up being a failure within a year. The reason is the lack of knowledge of the field. They feel the degrees they have earned and the certificates are enough to start a business. How to run a business without knowing anything about their line of business.

Some businesses are seasonal businesses and are for a period of time only. **For example** are the refrigeration business, solar panel business, operate for six months. But the loan installments, salary of staff and electricity bills have to be paid every month. Our needs are to be met each month. How can we meet them without business?

Some of them are based on raw materials. They can be run so long as the raw material is available. **For example**, coconut fiber manufacturing factories, fly ash brick factories, and there are many such examples. These are the difficulties arising because we focus only on the success aspect when commencing our business.

The victorious persons whom we come across are not suddenly victorious. They have tasted success after struggling, learning lessons, and after gaining knowledge. When we such persons we merely see their success. We don't see the struggles they have taken to taste such success. Here the victory is the apex of an iceberg top. The base of the iceberg and the surroundings are immersed in water. We merely see the visible apex. We feel that we too can create such a situation wherein the apex which is on the top of the mountain appears small. But for the apex to sustain, there needs to be a strong foundation which has been built over time, and created from failures, experiences and various other activities, which we don't see and many times we are unable to see the same.

Ok. how does on gain the subject knowledge? My humble opinion is that you need to work for a minimum of three years in a small enterprise which works on the field of business that you are aspiring to create. I repeat you need to work only in a small organization. Do you know the sort of person my father is? What a great man he was and the how rich he was? How can I work in a small organization? My friends work in a large organization in an air-conditioned cabin with a high salary. They have a bike and car etc., how can I work in a small organization? I can hear your angry questions above. Listen without anger, I will answer each of your questions.

You need to work in a small organization. The large organization that you see has arisen also from a smaller organization and they are doing multiple business at a later date. Then they can work in unrelated businesses as well. But they have gained their knowledge and experience from a smaller organization. TATA and Ambani have come up from a small organization. You too can become a TATA and Ambani. But for now you can create one only from small organizations. When you work for a large organization, you will be a small part of a Large Machine. When you work for a small organization, there are lots of opportunities to learn from the entire business. You can see all other departments, how they functioning.

Ok let's come to your **father**. Your father might be an honorable, rich person who is wealthier than the owner of that small organization. But is your father an entrepreneur? Does he have the basic business experience? And what is his business knowledge? that he has acquired. Failure or success is not an issue. Has he conducted any small business in his past? Then you can follow him which is not wrong too.

Let us come to your **friends**. You can join the job that your friends have joined in, which I don't refute. You can live in affluence like them by procuring a car and bike. But what do you wish to be 20 years from now. Do you wish to work in another large organization in a senior position? It is not wrong. Nothing wrong in going for a job. But by working in a large organization, do you wish to be a mere aspect of a larger Machine. If so you can continue. Nothing disrespectful job.

Don't you need a broad knowledge? Where can you obtain it, it can be gotten from a smaller organization only. You can gain knowledge from the various departments there. You can learn the entire organization from an eagle's view point. But you don't get that chance in a larger organization. Then go to the industrial exhibitions relating to your field as visitor and then participate in the same. Then you can understand the current business practices. The persons in that field of business would have written books on their respective fields. Get those books and read them. Join the debates they conduct. Learn by spending a bit of money. Only investment reaps income. The money spent on learning is an investment.

## Goal and Plan

We would have learnt from a few when learning to swim that when you close your eyes and jump into waters, one can reach the opposite shore. During swimming classes, certain persons push us and when required save us as well. That is the way many MSMEs start. Some wrong guidance is seen like the persons who push us into water. But here there are no persons to save us. There is no way to reach the shore. But many repeatedly jump into the same.

All of us live with the expectation of victories. What is victory in life? Is it a happy life or a healthy life? Is it a rich life or a combination of all the three? Which do you deem as victory? Likewise what is business success? What is your goal? Do you wish to earn a million from your business life? Else do you wish to earn a million per year? If you say money is not your aim, do you wish to employ many? Or do you wish employ millions of persons? Or do you wish to start a large organization that benefits millions? Or do you wish to combine all the three? Which is victory? And what your goal is? First determine your goal and then the plan will follow automatically. If you embark on a journey without knowing your goal you won't reach the destiny, if at all you reach the place it won't be on time.

For example, if you embark towards Delhi, you have to decide before you start right? when do you want to reach the place? What time do you want to reach? are the thoughts we have. Depending on the time at hand, we determine the start of journey the number of days, the mode of transport, is it via ground or air, is it a through journey? a straight journey? Do we stay on the route somewhere? What are the luggage? The cost involved, so many questions should arise.

Only if such questions arise you reach the correct destination on time. Else you will be merely thinking in a closed room else you will be repeating to your friends about your going to Delhi and whiling away your time.

If you don't determine the goal, the plan won't follow, and without planning there won't be a journey. You can't attain your goal without a journey and merely by resting. The victorious plan the journey and attain the goal. But we think of it as an easy growth and that they built a fortress. It is like what I earlier mentioned about the tip of an iceberg? It is not wise to speak of it without knowing the base of the iceberg. We may think they are victorious because of good luck. You might think of them as fools. There is no chance of their growing it is merely a luck.

He is less educated than me. He is of lower intelligence, and born of an ordinary family, he cannot think like me. I have the capacity for prognosticating the course of America, while he can't even locate America. You might have such thoughts.

He might be a fool like you think, but an intelligent person without a plan can be defeated by a fool with a plan. That is bound to happen. He never thought of defeating you. He never thought about you too. He determined his goals and asked the others about what he was ignorant about, and based on a planning of what to do next, he arrived at Delhi. You might be knowing America, but that is not the goal. We need to go to Delhi. Which is your goal. With a proper planning the person who goes to Delhi will one day go to America as well. You have not planned merely because you are aware of presidents, cities, bullet trains and Boeings in

America, due to which you have not even gone to the neighboring street.

**Planning and goal** are twin children. It is a double barrel gun. It is a twin ox-cart, it is parallel tracks, and we can state many more such examples. I can state all. It needs to be registered in your mind to that extent. There are persons who define the goal and plan separately. But we need to combine them is what I claim. At times despite planning we might have situation to detour, If we have a fixed goal, we can review our goal and confirm journey, when we have detoured we can approach our goal again and maintain our travel right method.

When during a voyage, due to enjoyment of it, the ship may detours, we search for the lighthouse and correct our course to reach the shores. Likewise we need to move the organization.

## Ignorance of Market Situation

Can we approach the market without knowing the market realities? If we do so the market will mock us. Most MSMEs start with the wrong information and guidance.

Market awareness will decide the sort of service and product to be marketed and the place of the same. You might ready to offer the best product or service. But what is the demand. Will most persons benefit from it? Who will buy a useless service or product? Why have we started a business or why should we start one.

It is for making money. Where do we get money? Is it from trees? Or from the oceans. Is it from air? Not at all. It is always from another person. Are you sarcastic to say that it comes from a large organization to the bank account? That is the reply for you. The person signing the check is also a human. The person depositing directly in the bank too is a human. Why should a person give you his life time savings? Why a money entrusted to someone should be given to you? Do you need the reason?

Your product or service should be useful to him or to his organization. Will you pay someone without any requirement? Demand moves everything. We need to manufacture the product in demand and then sell it. We need to supply the service or product that is in demand. Only based on demand is a product positioned in the market.

There is a philosophical song of **Vallalar** saying "I opened a shop but there were no buyers". What he wished to say was, he has stated sadly that the knowledge he wishes to dispense has no qualified recipients. The ones who think for people, think of their benefits.

But if we view from a business view point, if we advertise a useless product, none is going to buy it. Sometimes, your intention might be good, but does it satisfy the market demand is the basic question. There is no compulsion that the product or service of yours is going to sell just because your intentions are great, like your quality is good or that you have put in a lot of hard work. That is the sale is based on the need of the product to the public.

The reason Tata Nano car, Nokia cells, and Konica film rolls failed was due to unawareness of the demand. The reason for their disappearance is not recognizing the time based demands and the market demand. Perhaps some might require it, we need to consider whether that quantity of sale is enough for the continual operation of that organization.

So when large organizations can struggle, what are the mistakes of MSMEs? Let us see. When can we produce a product befitting our education and to commence a business befitting our training. Thinking of starting a business that someone has succeeded in some other town, starting a business to where one produces a product to supply to an organization that requires the product, rather all those products that don't consider the market requirements lead to failure of such industries. Industries that disregard the market requirements are bound to lose.

## Depending on Government Schemes

Government schemes, offers, aid, and loans don't help in running a business. Don't think I am into antigovernment speech. All that is required. But I am stating that for an entrepreneur who thinks he can start a business merely with that. The additional points in a video games can discount our defeat, but cannot ensure success. The government schemes and offers are to ensure that the MSMEs don't close down with time due to the untimely mistakes they commit. I have detailed this in the next paragraph, read this again and understand the same.

No industry can be successful, if it is designed based on the amount of Government loans. What is your Project Cost? When such a question is asked, most MSMEs state the maximum value of the government loan schemes.

How can everyone have a standard vest size? How can everyone have a standard slipper size?

How can someone build a similar house in different plot sizes?

Government scheme is meant for all kinds of persons. There are many reasons for the issue of a certain scheme we don't need to discuss that. But how does the government classify the schemes. It is designed in a way that it helps many entrepreneurs and reaches them, and based on certain points. It is not necessary that it fits every individual. Each business is of a different size. The plot size, the working hours, number of staff, equipment type and numbers, the electrical capacity of the equipment, wages, overheads, number of rooms, monthly expenses, time period of business operations, capital expenses, are the many parameters. Based on that the planning and estimation of each business differs. Hence the Project Cost is never based on the maximum permissible government loan schemes. If so are these schemes a non-necessity. If you ask thus, I would say such a question is useless.

I have stated earlier that most start-ups slide down and it doesn't run as per our prediction. Many parameters such as some ups and downs, unforeseen accidents, downward sales, change of market state, change of time period, unavailability of raw materials, reduction in demand, can affect the business. Government Schemes are offered to the extent that such hindrances for the entrepreneur can be corrected.

Hence we should not design the business based on the Government loan scheme, first we should design our business and then based on the apropos government scheme, we should utilize the same.

On the contrary if we design our business as per the government schemes, it is like walking in an ill-fitting shoes. Many MSMEs lose this way. Based on government schemes the outlay is increased and based on loans the outlay is being reduced. Here we should realize that our goal is to design a business that is going to be long lasting and is not meant for procuring a government scheme. The government aid is a mere additional prize. Hence let us move towards a successful business by designing one which gives profits and incorporates the latest technology.

## Financial Management

We can write many thousand pages on financial management. But what we wish to share is based on the mistakes committed by MSMEs.

Most MSMEs when spoken to about financial management state, how to manage the finances when one doesn't have the same? But financial management is created from the time of thinking of running a business to creating a project report.

Everyone is aware that the first deviation is a total deviation. The mistake in project report is bound to last for the entire business time period.

In the previous heading we spoke about designing a business as per the government schemes. Read it again, all mistakes of financial management happen there. All MSMEs state the value of the equipment and installations when asked about planning outlay. If asked about the capital to start business, they say that if I were to buy that equipment, I would somehow be victorious.

What is the expenses incurred in starting a business? What is the future plan? The idle cost incurred. What is the plan at that time? How much should one apportion for raw materials?

What is the wages? What is the overheads? The marketing costs. The advertisement costs, and many others need to be considered. When doing so each aspect should be accounted for so that we can estimate the correct requirements. But financial management is handling some other kind of money. By estimating properly we can merely know the precise requirement. But expending that is a different work. We need to expend the money that is apportioned for a certain job. It should not be deployed elsewhere. If it is known that it will be spent for something else, it should be considered in accounting beforehand. Despite acting as per our action plan, there are bound to be mistakes. Under this situation, if we spend for an unplanned product or action, we need to face the consequences.

If the product or action is within a business, it doesn't matter. Even the minor mistakes can spoil the profits in a planned business. But if we spend towards an unplanned product or action, we cannot even imagine the disaster. Most MSMEs act this way. They get a loan for a business and think of buying a car.

That too for used cars, buying a new car by itself is wrong, why talk of a used car. I have been cheated oh God! Still others use that money for marriages. Such business or marriages don't succeed either. Blind decisions never lead to victory. Can we run a business depending on the marriage gift money ("Moi" in Tamil)? Who knows how much might come in? Only what we have given someone else is going to return back to us. If don't do that basic calculation, what can we do. Enough of examples. The lesson to be learnt from this is the money apportion for a purpose should be spent for that purpose.

OK. This is based on the money on hand or the money gotten from others. But there is a financial institution called the bank. Each MSME has a fear of approaching bank. Any MSME entrepreneur is scared to approach a bank. What will they enquire about? Which aspects will they enquire about? But when entering a bank if we feel like criminals and the bank staff as police, how will our talk succeed. But the same persons get a loan at 10% per month and doing business. But they are not scared of the creditor who are receiving 10% interest per month.

There is no hesitancy, will he give? Won't he give? Is a suspicion that doesn't come? There is a courage that we can approach another creditor in case of refusal. But why do we have this fear of banks. Why don't we have the confidence that we can approach another bank in case the present bank refuses us? Because the main reasons are ignorance of the bank, and the financial management network.

Like I mentioned before, if were to note down each cost of the business, estimate the income, deduct the pre-estimated costs, and if we understand that the balance amount can be used for repaying the principal and interest and if this is conveyed to the bank, we can definitely obtain a loan. For he too is looking for another person like us.

To the extent we believe that we can convince a creditor who offers loans at a rate of 10% per month, why don't we have the confidence to convince the bank that offers loans at a rate of 1% per month. This is because of the ignorance about banks.

Left to me banks and creditors are the same. There is only one difference, the bank gives a low interest loan and the creditor does so at a higher rate. That is all. Both will threaten in case of non-payment. But if you repay properly both will like to give you another loan.

The reason for mishandling the bank is due to ignorance of financial management. List each aspect of the loan that you are to receive or you wish to receive to the bank manager. He needs to understand that there is profit enough to repay the loan in your business. Is it stable? Is there no technological hindrances? If the bank understands the above issues? they will help you in various occasions. They will also give you explanations on how to get a loan.

We might misunderstand something and try to hide it from the bank, this leads to many issues. Many banks have a different perspective of the government schemes. Since many banks and debtors discuss the subsidy of the willful defaulter beforehand, they don't handle the person in a straight forward manner. If one keeps discussing subsidy, the bank thinks that he has structured his loan only to get the subsidy. Left to me, if irrespective of the Subsidy, if the project report is structured based on the real profits as I mentioned earlier, the Bank staff himself will counsel on what type of financial assistance to procure. Rather if you were to discuss when you will get the subsidy directly with the bank staff, they feel your aim is merely to obtain a subsidy. For him, you are not the first person they have come across. They interact with many persons who are doing business in that area. Many entrepreneurs of that area might have a bank account there. They know pretty well how the entrepreneurs discuss and how the potential debtors wishing a subsidy discuss. Bear in mind that they meet many persons like yourself. The business project report should cover all aspects you need to prove that the project report contains the three below features.

1. Gives profits in any situation

2. There are no technological issues

3. It is stable till the time period of repayment of loans

It should not prioritize the subsidy rather the above three features for the aid is an additional protection, and not the main reason. Businesses that don't consider the subsidy rather only the profits will have many venues of success and the doors of many banks will be open as well.

If the bank refuses loans despite all those being correct, the bank might perhaps be a wrong one. You don't need to worry about that. Contact another bank without reservations. Not all banks act the same. If one lets you down, others will help you. For there are total of 120,000 bank branches in India.

## Preplanning and Due Registration

After barter system lead to the money system industries were created. Basically industry implies not a building, rooms, the products, manager or yourself. It is some papers, means documents, registrations etc. It is irrespective of the size or nationality of the organization.

There are office less organizations, there are transport organizations without their own vehicles. There are organizations that cannot deposit cash in the cash box daily by hand. But there are no organizations without some documents or registrations as I mentioned, if these don't exist, there is no organization. If so it is a mere shop.

They are no organizations, they don't get government approvals. If so, there can be several future confusions.

Any MSMEs, any impex organization, it is the government that controls them.

There are many registrations, such as license, registrations, bank accounts, PAN, organization law registrations, registration for export and import, electricity and land records, etc.

98% of the MSMEs in India don't register themselves as a MSME I have seen many operation with a SB account rather than a current account. I have met many organizations in real estate that don't operate via bank. I have seen ones operating without PAN. There are many more procedural errors, record errors etc. They merely say on outside that they are conducting business. But all of those are on the wrong track. Due to this our journey will be delayed. There will be unnecessary confusions. It will create a situation of non-availability of loans for further growth. I have written the following lessons as to which registration will come under a certain serial order.

Read and understand them. It needs to be definitely mentioned as a challenge, hence I have registered the same here.

## English

Please don't ask "I came here to learn a business and he is teaching me language". Under the title of Challenges, English is a challenge for MSMEs entrepreneurs it needs to be mentioned. It has to be spoken of here.

Whether you like it or not English is the global language. It is the main business language. It is the official language and adjunct language of many world governments and countries. Most industrial and technological terms are in English. The current industrial terms are in English. But I won't say that unless you have a literary English knowledge, one cannot do business. I know that even illiterate person have tasted success. Educated persons can be employed and one can run the business effectively and attain success. There is a way for that. But for fast growth in business one needs English. I never said one needs English literary knowledge. I am not even saying about spoken knowledge. If one can read out word for word, it is enough. Then one can understand the meaning easily.

English is vital for computers, cells, and modern equipment, the future belongs to paperless business. To contact others and for others to know our details, the registration Number of organizations and personal registration all contain English. In a multilingual country like India, to each person his language is superior. But what is superior is not important now. The current aim is to ensure speedy business growth. Then we have to communicate in English which is the global business language.

In discussing communication, you have scared me. Why should you get panicky on needing to learn English? No language is superior. Nothing is inferior. All of them is human created and by ordinary humans like us. These are flesh and blood humans. They are no golden. We don't feel hesitant, inferior or scared on ignorance of some other language. But English is designed as an intellectual language hence the ones ignorant of English are deemed as fools in our society. But we don't need to worry about that. It is enough if we know some words. Then it is enough if we can learn word by word.

If we can speak, it is strength. A habit of learning to speak another language is like adding another friend and is empowering. Hence learn it as small words. Then practice writing bigger words. That is it, English will cease to be a challenge for persons like us in MSMEs.

## Chapter 3

# Why Should Start Business?

Why should we start a business? We have already commenced one. If you have such question in your mind, Aspirants, Write down why should you start a business? Existing ones, Please review by writing down, are you on the right track? But in my perspective even if it is existing, one should write down and treat it like a new organization.

For why have most MSMEs started? How did they do so? These are the points that are seldom thought of. Those without any core values don't exist for long, but business needs to be permanent has to live for long time. You can take stable decisions only in long lasting business. Hence we should know why we should commence business. Let it take one hour or one day, don't commence a business without writing this down. If it is existing, review how the business intent originated and the original intent should be recognized.

As per the world, this is an Entrepreneurship Era. Now a days, Globally, The ones who talk about entrepreneurship they discuss the basic traits as passion, and superior thinking, best idea, solution through business.

But most of Indian MSMEs don't originate that way. Till 30 years they think of government jobs, take efforts, they prepare for various government jobs, they waste their youth over government jobs, then after 35 years for private jobs, then for overseas jobs, and finally having exhausted their options, and based on situation and for livelihood, and to live on an everyday basis, and to make money, to survive, they think of business as the last option, which is the mindset of most Indians.

Our country has all the wrong notions of money such as earning money is greed, it is the source of all evil, money alone is not life, one cannot be victorious over everything with money, and money is not everything. Though most persons across the globe have such traits, most of them are Indians and the ones who have misunderstood the Indian concept, have such superstitions.

Everyone needs money but they believe that it leads to evil, lots of money breeds evil, and good persons don't accumulate wealth.

But I am a good person and won't harm others. But I need money. These are the confusing thoughts faced by many MSME entrepreneurs. When we move towards a goal, our thoughts and actions should be same.

Money is not evil. No money does evil things to others by itself. There is nothing such as good or bad money. Money is just a tool. First we need to understand that when it is in the hands of the good persons it breeds good and in the hands of evil, it leads to evil.

As I mentioned before first seek the answer to the basic question of why should I start a business and write it down. Then read to repeatedly. What I mentioned at the start of the book is the basis for victory. We need to determine the goal. Only if we know the intent, we can think of a goal. Only if we know the goal can we plan to move towards the same.

Is it by choice or by compulsion that we have come to business? Or is it because of passion that we have come to business? Or Is it because we have learnt some industrial knowledge?

Just because we had the education in some industry that initiated you to start this business? You need to raise these questions and get to know the reason for coming in to your business. It might be a wrong reason, never mind. We can correct the same after you found that only. To write down the reason for entering into business shall shape the future planning.

Ok. we have found the reasons. Now are you an entrepreneur? Or a business man, don't confuse yourself with that. Don't confuse yourself about the industry. Who are you in the field of business? Are you

Unable to understand, is it manufacturing or service. You have not asked the nature of business. Now are you an entrepreneur or business man. Search the answer to these questions.

Still unable to understand? By asking in details, there is nothing new in the product which would be sold by the business man. There is nothing new in the product involved in trade or the one sold in the market as per the needs of the market.

But an entrepreneur is not just one creates a product. He creates a business. Is he creating a business? Yes he is creating a business. You need to think of market needs. It is the demand that determines the business as I mentioned before.

I am not refuting that. But at times an entrepreneur has the capacity to change the market demand as per his intent.

**For Example,** in most houses idli is consumed as breakfast. Those going out for work and those without time to prepare a breakfast, or those who skip breakfast due to work constraint, are the customers for this idli business. Business man who want to sell idlis to these people bought from someone else, is trader. He can get the idlis from someone and sell it. Or He may himself steam boil the same and spray water, and can place each idli on a plate and sell it. Are you hungry? Let us eat later. Idli is not an invention of this person, he merely understood the market demand for idli. Hence he is selling it and hence he is a businessman.

**For Example**, The mango fruit from kodaikanal is very sweet. It is one of the three important fruits of Tamilnadu. It has low sugar and ore sweetness. It quenches thirst and hunger. But you don't get it at all times. It is not found in every town. None can dislike it. If such a person exists, he might not have tasted it. The business man is one who supplies the mango fruit to one who demands it, as in this case. He has realized the market demand and human hunger and he procures and sells them, hence he is a businessman. All fruits get spoilt, and mango too gets spoilt. Apart from the ones sold, the rest may get spoilt. It can get rotten.

Here an **entrepreneur** is created. He has tastes mangoes. He has realized the love of people for mangoes. He knows it can get rotten. He knows that if it can preserved, it can be supplied to everyone at all times. He juices the mangoes, and adds sweetening agent, and cold stores them and he feels that if he supplies them at all times to various countries, he can satisfy that demand, and he feels that he can earn lots of income via that, and creates something new, and earns an income, such a person is an **entrepreneur**. Mango is not his product, mango juice is not new to this word, one who knows the method of preserving and comes forward to preserve, and refrigerate and supply it across the world, is an entrepreneur.

**In this situation, why have we started or why should we start? Find out if you have such a question. Apply to this mango story also.**

Let me state **another example**, five of us entrepreneurs got together and went to the central portion of Tamil Nadu to a certain town. We were journeying to find a place for a new factory.

There is a lot of onion produced in that town. We were journeying with the intent of creating an onion storage and to gather information in that town. One of my co travelers has a shrimp farm and belongs to a seaside town. Others belong to various other places. After our lunch we were standing to wash our hands. There was no water in the tap. We got the ground water from a sump to wash our hands. We gargled our mouth and were washing our hands. One of the persons had told us that the water is very salty and not to drink it. Still we gargled our mouths and washed our hands. But the person who gargled last is the person who hails from the seashore town. He looked at me and smiled. He smiled and said, this town is not a seaside town, but this water contains salt for shrimp cultivation. Hence if we start a shrimp farm here, we can cultivate good quality shrimp in this town which is not close to the seaside and one can also sell the shrimp at the neighboring towns for a lower rate. I would say that this is the qualification of an entrepreneur. We all found the brine to be a nuisance, but he found it to be an opportunity. He immediately started to construct a business in that town.

**You can find the answer to the question of "why one should start a business". Did you get it here?**

Search and you will find it, read it till you get it again and again. Then you will understand.

Unless you get an answer to why you need to start a business, do not get into any kind of business. Don't think of the next job. If you get the answer why you need to start a business, ask yourself if you fit into the same and if you can work with full commitment, and then arrive at a decision. First decide and then slowly plan to start a business. Let us seen in the next section, how to start a business.

## Chapter 4

# How to Start a Business?

The idea of starting a business might have entered our minds in any possible way. Due to compulsion of time, in the heat of the moment when you read a book such as this, seeing scenes in a movie where the hero attains a lot of business success, seeing the rapid business growth of others, something must have motivated you and planted the idea of business in your mind. The idea of starting a business might have entered our minds in any possible way, but you cannot start a business in any possible way. There is a procedure for the same. There is an order for the same.

Learn the sections on why they fail and why one should start a business several times or read all sections till you understand them completely, then you get the solution to the question of how to start a business.

First decide on the type of industry. In the first section, I have classified the industry into seven types. You need to decide on the industry to you wish to enter. It comes under 7 types and 3 subtypes. They are Manufacturing, Service and Trade. I have explained the three separately.

Basically no government encourages **trade businesses**. For they are not directly our industry. We cannot decide the price, any industry where we cannot set the price is not our industry is my opinion. Further it encourages brokers. It leads to false price rise in the market. Also because of this, the government doesn't encourage trade. Hence ensure that your industry comes under manufacturing or service.

## Don't Copy

Don't copy others industry when selecting. It might seem that some person has been victorious in a business due to some reason. Don't chose the same industry blindly. Some of them end up choosing the same industry or something similar to the same. Some might have been successful despite copying the same. The ones who commence with due planning, take into account the various business environments, understand the nooks and corners, and take their steps. But the ones who copy the business, are like the trailer in a vehicle.

When the front vehicle turns, the trailer turns and when the first speeds, the latter too speeds. There is a chance of the front vehicle stopping at a speed breaker. There is a chance of the trailer colliding. If you were to copy the existing business model there is a chance of the preexisting business person losing along with you. For you are going to share his customers. You are going to spoil yourself and the preexisting person. There is a chance of the bank refusing you a loan by duly considering all of these factors when you approach a bank for loan.

The experience gained by the former person is something you might not have. Your lack of experience and not matching his speed will lead to your instability in the market. There is a saying that an extinguishing candle glows brighter. If you see him in the final stages where he is shing bright and you decide to start a similar business, he will be likely planning the end, but you will be merely starting. There is a chance that this will take you down the wrong direction. The first deviation will lead to a total deviation. The equipment he has purchased might be apropos to the time period. But if you were to copy the same, and buy an equipment, it might not fit the current period. If in the final stages he upgrades to the latest technology, you cannot match his competition.

Hence choose a unique business, take a decision on who your customers are. I don't mean the individual count of the customers. Take them as a group. For instance men, and women sportspersons aged 12–50 years are the regular customers of the sports shop. In a hair cutting shop, any male between the ages of 2 onwards is a customer. In a saree shop all married women are customers and there is bound to be competition. Hence you need to have a unique selling point. Each line of this section is important. Read it repeatedly.

## Types of Industry

As I mentioned before, industry is of three types. They are service, trade and Manufacturing. I have taken each of them separately and explained it below.

### Service Industry

You have decided to start a **hairdressing shop**, is it meant for women, men, and children or for everyone or is it unisex? Is it merely a hair cutting salon or a hair dressing salon? What is the age group of persons are your target? Will those aged 60 years and above turn up. Will the parents come with teenage Person? Are there enough customers in the area where you are opening a shop? Is there another rival shop there? If so why should his customers come to you? How to change them over from that shop to yours? You need to research each and every point and start.

### Trade Industry

You are thinking of starting a **stationery shop**. Who are the customers, are they students, teachers, government officers, or private employees, where are you going to start a shop. Does it contain customers for your products? Are there organizations from which there can be a permanent purchase made. Will you get the contract from government organizations? What are the basic qualifications to participate in the event of tender?

Do you have those? Can you meet the demanded capacity at one shot? Can you do so in the specified time period? If the wrong product has been purchased can you render an exchange of goods or return of cash? What is the time period you have set for goods exchange? You need to research each and every point and start.

**Manufacturing Industry**

Let us take the **plastic injection molding industry.** Many plastic equipment can be produced in this industry. Hence are we going to produce the product needed for industry? Is it going to be for households? Or are we going to manufacture children's toys. Are we going to both produce and sell? If we are going to sell, which is our market. What is our marketing experience? Are you going to start a retail? Are you are going to distribute to other sales persons. Is it for local market? Or for out of station other than local markets? Is it for exports to overseas? You need to research each point and start.

## Selecting the Product for Sale

**OK,** we have seen the details of each service, Manufacturing and trade with an example. What are you going to do? Is it from Manufacturing, trade or service? Are you going to produce something, are you going to provide service. You need to do that first. When selecting the product for sale, it can be goods, it can be a service product.

Only by selling them will you get cash. Hence that is your product for sale. You need to select that first. You need to know that first.

I speak in various entrepreneur development programs. After the program many of them interact with me personally. Many of them are from 20–45 years of age who meet with me. They ask me to suggest a product that sells well. I ask them immediately if they are to going run the business or myself. They tell me that they are going to run a business but they ask me to select the product and they will go by my suggestions. I don't know them. It won't even be 10 minutes since I started speaking. How can I select a business for them? There are no plug and play model business in world. Even for a franchisee model you have to analyze that will it be suitable for you in all aspects.

Still others ask me for a profitable business. Am I a person of breakthrough? Even the flagship Nokia organization is walking a path towards your town. All businesses can lead to either profits or losses. It is nothing to do with the industry. There are many other reasons. Read the chapter again on why MSMEs originate.

The choice of a product for sale can be based on your education, industry knowledge, market demand, industrial need, the capital levels, and your time.

Another curse of our nation is **caste**.

Since the caste is linked to a business it too influences the choice of a business. Since some works cannot be done by us, we treat them as low grade ones and since others might look down upon us we don't select such industries.

Some others have a caste benefit. Since there might not be any competition, it is selected and is done over many years as a group without any current update and research. Hence there is nothing novel about such industry, and continues unchanged.

Which product can we select, can we do it so continuously. Is it profitable? Can it fulfill the current market demands?

We need to consider this before selecting a product for sale.

## Permanent Account Number (PAN)

After selecting the product, you need to get a PAN, Most account holders have a PAN. If it is not so, request for one. Some feel they are starting a new and small business, why should I go for a PAN.

They think that there will be government hassles due to PAN. Left to me it is a useless fear.

Currently you cannot start a bank account with PAN. Get a PAN in your name either after or before you start a business. The government offers PAN for a low fees. Some private organizations get you a PAN for a low fees of few hundred. Not just bank account, all industries require a PAN. There is no hassles because of this so long as you don't create any mistakes. Do you or need money. Do you need earn duly or not. If so get a PAN.

## Udyog Aadhar Number – UAN

PAN is used to unify the bank accounts of an individual. An individual is given an Aadhar No. the government allots the UAN. Every industry requires an UAN mandatorily. For which the government has created UAN. Most industries don't mandate this UAN. But for us who are in the MSME, the government has planned and allotted this UAN. Further in our nation many MSMEs are functioning.

Like I mentioned earlier, there are persons who are scared to get a PAN and register with the government. Similarly in MSMEs nearly 94% of the persons are unregistered. As of the year 2015, 2196902 persons have registered as MSME as per the MSME Act of 2006. Since the details are inadequate, most industries are no classified, the information of all states and UTs are not unified. After the year 2015, the government ordered that the UAN has to be mandatorily registered. It should contain the name of the proprietor, age, Caste, bank AC, PAN, mobile No, residential address, office address, factory address, name of the industry, and Number etc. are being aggregated. Based on the industrial and caste classification, many offers are made by the government. That is the second thing we need to procure and register namely the UAN. Currently, it is mandatory that only if you have UAN, a bank account can be created.

For getting a UAN, one needs a PAN and cell number linked to it along with AADHAR No and a bank account number. It can be a savings account as well. Go to the site udyogaadhar.gov.in, and register it. It is designed in the self-declaration mode. There is no office or official for this. Hence you don't need to pay any one and get cheated. It is a free service. There is no registration charges. Some false websites, after registering demand money. But in the site udyogaadhar.gov.in money is not demanded finally. Each person can create five UAN. Means to say the government has given the opportunity of creating five different industries for the MSMEs.

## Bank Account

The next is the bank account No. it is our mode of getting money. The above two documents, our photo ID, A residence proof, can be used for creating a current account. Most of them are ignorant of the Current account. When you tell them to do so, they have unwanted fears and they are hesitant to create a current account. It is a mode of depositing money by depositing the check obtained from a large organization and written in the name of your organization. If the account is not in the name of your organization, you need to understand that most organizations will not be willing to give you an opportunity. To run a business in a savings account will create a situation of starting at a low level and finishing our lives at a lower level.

If you run a business via savings account, it won't be deemed as a business. **No large organization will be willing to offer you business nor can you get a government orders**. Hence a current account is very important. Later when you approach the banks for your schemes, it will be very useful. To move to the next level, current account is very important. That is all.

If you have these three documents, it implies that you are ready for business.

Now you can start your business without fears. You can take the checks in your organization's name and deposit them. The business that you start with the three documents is called proprietorship organization. With this you can do business without fears.

When several such organizations get together it is called, partnership, private limited, public limited, and many others. These have to be duly registered, submit the documents, and then you can start a bank account. Hence, I would recommend a proprietorship organization in order to easily start and run a business.

# Chapter 5

# Marketing

**Marketing** is the introduction of a product or service in a way that a business is commenced and ready for sale, in a way that is available for the customer, or in a way that they become familiar with the product.

Not just MSMEs even large organizations are brought down by this challenge of marketing.

After commencing a business, if we take a deep breath and relax saying we have completed our job, our story too ends that way. Our job is not yet over. Truly our job starts there. We should not relax. We should be ready to run. Do we have the persons to abide by our commands like that of an owner of a large organization? No. Nor do we have large sums of money. If so we can delegate our marketing responsibilities to some marketing agency and lie back and relax. We can appoint an MBA graduate, who has specialized in marketing from some large management institute and lie back and relax and monitor him. Even such large organizations are successful in marketing, by daily classes, marketing teams, many point details, and many other tools. But MSMEs like us are not in that state.

Hence we should take every step with due caution. Most MSME entrepreneurs consider commuting to the office everyday as a great effort. We don't even inform the others of the product and service that we offer. They think a name board outside the organization is enough. They think people will flock to their place by default. The name board in the entrance is a mere tool to ensure the people who seek you attain you correctly.

Can you start a business only with a name board? May be it may prove useful in the daily provision shop in a market. It may be helpful for some trade business. Large organizations which are like selling products in small shops may benefit from this. It may be useful for some grocery shops and the public will seek them out. Even groceries can be ordered through online (**Apps**) and will reach you the next day.

They don't print a visiting card. Even those who do so don't have an email address. That is the current state of most MSMEs. Most type out an email address for the sake of visiting card, they don't even bother to login to the email. We need to go in the direction of the world. Abide by the world is what I need to repeat.

## Smart Phones

In the last section I concluded that you can start a business only if you have a PAN, UAN, and a bank AC.

But you can add a smart phone to it. The owners of MSMEs that procure a smart phone don't do so for themselves. I don't mean the young entrepreneurs. I meant the age group of 35–40 years. Most of the aspirants start an MSME by 30–35 years. I have explained the reasons earlier. First I would recommend a smart phone. An email address helps you enter a large network of websites.

Also add a cell phone. MSMEs are sole proprietorship organizations. It helps the sole proprietor to market. The lack of PC will be resolved using a **smart phone**. A PC will be even more useful. Where the world is shrunk, what if you alone were to belong to another world. Ok getting a **smart phone** is good. That is it.

## Types of Industries

We have classified industries earlier. We have classified the industries as per the activity. Now we will classify them on the basis of **customers**.

Who are your customers? The place full of customers is a customer. Hence you can classify your customers like Business to customers B2C, Business to business B2B, and Business to government B2G and Business to exports B2E. So you are unable to understand. Let me explain each of them below.

## Business to Customer (B2C)

The product you manufacture is directly useful to an individual or reaches a customer directly which is called business to customer or B2C.

For example, **clothes, foods, decoration items, books, footwear, sports goods,** are procured directly by individuals for their uses. Such products are manufactured, sold or manufactured and sold are called the business to customer or B2C. Here market is all the individuals in the world. All of the basic requirements of people such as food and clothing come under business to customer or B2C.

## Business to Business (B2B)

If your industry is useful to some other industry it is called the business to business B2B. Not all industries can function as stand alone. Each requires the help of the other. Offering a product or service that is useful to another business or a product or service that is created by a business to another business is called Business to business or B2B.

For example if you were to produce bicycle seats then your industry is useful to another industry and is called a Business to business or B2B. Even if you create a gear wheel for the same organization, it is called as Business to business or B2B.

Microsoft Corporation produces a product called the MS office and sells them. It also creates an operating system called Windows. These are beyond individuals and are meant for large organizations, this way Microsoft Corn. too is classified as a business to business or B2B. When they sell it to an individual it can also be classified as Business to customer or B2C. Most industries use the Microsoft products.

All industries have an office. All of them require stationaries. If you are into purchase and sales of stationeries it comes under business to business or B2B. This way the business to business or B2B persons have the opportunity of interacting directly with the owners of large businesses and establishing a permanent industry via a contract. But the danger is that when the organization is affected, you too will be affected.

### Business to Government (B2G)

**Here** government is our customer. Here the government is our direct or indirect customer. Finally we get the money from the government. Annually the Indian government spends nearly 7 lakh cores of rupees to run the Public works institutions. Apart from this the state expenses, the industries that we establish to receive the money etc from the state governments all fall under the Business to Government B2G.

Currently TATA corpn. takes up the passport services of the Indian Government and runs it.

Many Public Undertakings of the government of India such as BHEL, BEL, IOCL, BPCL, are directly into sales. They manufacture many products, and sell them. They are all industries run by the government. Like I mentioned earlier, they too cannot be stand alone. The requisites and equipment of these industries, can be met with by your organization which in this case is also called the Business to Government B2G.

## Business to Export (B2E)

The products created by some industries, are meant for overseas use. They are called Business to Export B2E. These industries have tax offers by the government too.

All industries into exports, are all large ones. When talking about MSME, why have we discussed exports is a question asked by many MSMEs. But it is wrong point. More than 40% of the export share belongs to the MSMEs is a truth that cannot be overseen. In world exports India's share is very less, we are only into 2% of the world exports. Hence exports is a large opportunity for MSMEs. Also if many MSMEs get into exports, we can cross 60% of the total exports.

The most important and possible aspect of exports is you don't need to search for lots of customers. Most of the export orders are bulk orders. They don't belong to piece meal business. Even with few customers we can achieve great heights within a short span of time. In exports, market implies all other nations except ours, and mostly there is no tax for exports.

Rather the Indian Government offers you incentives for exports. About 16000 items are sent via exports abroad, in which 6000 of them are via the MSMEs is a fact that builds additional confidence for MSMEs. It also lends confidence that we are helping improve the foreign exchange of the country.

## Logo and Motto

The logo implies your service and products, the actions and the nature of your organization and it is an image or feature. It can be an image or your organization's name in specific words. Some use the first letter of their organization. About logos we can write a large book, not just a small one. The logo that you have created either as an image, or writing should not change throughout the course of your operations. Motto implies the base line that you conceive, indicating the product or service of your organization, its quality, the explanation. When you convey the message via that base line which is simple and powerful enough to understand the nature of your organization, it gets imprinted deeply in the minds of the public or other organizations.

## Website

In the current linked world, a website is very important for all organizations. It suffices to have a website with four pages. Images, pictures, sounds etc can be used as required. The geolocation to locate your organization can be specified. The customers that get into your email can be sent a message directly.

The customers that view your website via cell phone have the chance of contacting you directly via your mobile. It helps give details of visitors to your website via social media. Once your ID is given, it is the current practice to search for your website to verify your presence. Hence create a website immediately.

## Business Card and Brochure

Ensure that your Business card contains, your business name, name of the organization, designation, mobile number, landline number, email address, website address, Office address, factory address, logo or emblem.

If the business card is a small note on your business, brochure is a handbook with details of your organization. The logo or emblem, the product details, the strength of your organization, the strength of your equipment, and service quality, certificates containing some narrations of your organization, are displayed with a few images in the brochure.

Routinely the email address, the website address, officer address, factory address, and telephone Number, cell number, landline number, mobile number, can also be indicated.

All of these should be ready before getting into the market. Hence I am mentioning each without fail, we should not enter the market without these.

The world is wide and contains implicit opportunities. The market is wide. We have seen all types. The Indian government offers many marketing opportunities to the MSMEs. From the year 2006 the Indian government has been taking many actions for the MSMEs and has been giving the apropos opportunities as well. They are the below.

## Government Tenders

The Indian government consists of 29 states, and 7 union territories. Our country has a population of about 40 crores. To run the government machinery there are many departments. The Indian government spends nearly 8 lakh crores of rupees annually to run the public institutions, the union government offices, ministries, and this amount is spent merely for operating the public distributions in terms of product and services. By offering the products and services, the Indian government has been running the government efficiently.

In the government procurement of 8 lakh crores, the Indian government has made reservations for the MSMEs. This includes 29 states and 7 union territories. The expenses for running these is a very large amount. The products and services rendered for this is just too much. Hence the Indian MSME should observe the above facts.

Ok let us come back to the Indian government. What are the opportunities offering to MSMEs in the procurement of ₹ 8 lakh crores?

The Indian government has created an act called the Public procurement Bill 2012. As per the Act, of the total products and services offered and procured by the Public institutions, 25% should come from the MSMEs. Sale orders of 25 lakh crores are ready for MSMEs. For the weaker sections of women, tribal and scheduled castes, of the 25% about 3 and 4% are allotted respectively.

To get the ₹ 2 lakh crores orders you should first get a UAN. Secondly you should get a digital signature, or DSC. DSC is offered for individuals and organizations separately. We need to get individual and organization DSCs, currently it is offered in a pen drive.

If you have these two, you have the doors of ₹ 2 lakh crores open to you. In the website **http://eprocure. gov.in/cppp,** the Indian government has organized it in a way that all the public institutions can release the contractual orders at one place. In a day about 700 contractual orders are coming out of each department.

If you have the products or services mentioned in them, you too can apply. All the information is released in the website. It is designed in an open way. It has a common design for all departments. It is has been designed to browse as per day, city, product or service. In case you have not started the industry, or you have thought of some industry, you can understand the market demand for your product or service via this website. You can design your business accordingly.

The startups can understand the issues relevant to public institutions via this website. You can get sufficient information on creating new products or services. MSMEs need not just keep browsing this site, rather they can also register in the separate website of the public institutions they have selected. Via that there can be a good relation between yourself and government officials. It gives the opportunity to participate in concluded contracts. It can also create opportunities wherein in the future you are consulted and additional contracts are designed.

The above are the opportunities of the Indian union government only. Apart from this 37 other governments are into India. They are all opportunities for B2G working for the Indian government.

## MSME Data Bank

The specific website **msmedatabank.in**, is where each MSME entrepreneur has to register the details of his industry after procuring the PAN and UAN. In this entrepreneur, associations and business finance institutions, each offer a separate entry and each is unified under a single umbrella, and in order to frame a scheme for MSME are gathering details. Since each member has a separate entry, MSMEs can select the correct procedure, and register their details. All details of the government schemes, are transmitted via your email.

## Government Electronic Market Place (GeM)

GOVERNMENT ELECTRONIC MARKET PLACE or GeM was started on September 6, 2018. From 6th of September to October 17th, 2018, it was operated by the Indian government, as a national institute, in order to unify all the central and state government departments, and as a patronage for MSMEs.

The website **http://gem.gov.in,** is operated so that the small amount of products that are daily procured by the governments, their departments, public institutions, can be obtained in a transparent manner from the MSMEs. This has been designed so that the outstanding amounts of closed tenders, and that don't come under the government contracts, and the products that are required separately, can be procured directly from the entrepreneur.

Before the September 2018, **DGS&D** (DIRECTORATE GENERAL OF SUPPLIES AND GOODS) was functional. Here a producer has to determine the price of his product on his own. That price list has to be sent to all the government institutions. By that the situation wherein different government institutions procure the same product for different prices in different areas is avoided. The price is determined annually once, and the price list submitted to the government once.

This has been designed such that a long time that is spent for the MSMEs to get a seller after participating in the tender process is avoided. Delay doesn't fit into all circumstances.

**If an equipment of BHEL NLC etc get dysfunctional,** if it takes a long time to repair, there will be tremendous losses. If a spare part or a equipment is being replaced, and under a situation where it will be compensated, the tenders are announced, and it will take minimum of 3 months to receive the item. But the situation will be very worse. For that as per the price list given by the **DGS & D** if we were to purchase the product, and fit it and immediately compensate the losses. We can also buy separate spare parts.

The same **DGS & D** has changed to **GeM** and with web development it further gives some more opportunities. Now the situation of changing and deciding on the price annually once doesn't exist. **GeM** can change the price as and when it requires. The entrepreneur can register by himself the product images, details, prices, and notes at any time. Just like a direct auction, the auction amount can be increased. Any price that you quote is the inclusive **GST**. Hence when we decide the prices, please do so carefully. It is not a situation that once the price is given, you cannot change it later.

You can change it whenever you feel like. But you cannot change the price after the sale order.

The seller identity won't be known to anyone. Only the item, its price and the information given by you will be revealed. Even the organization name won't be displayed. For the government officials, in order to avoid partiality and corruption, has designed it in such a way.

Across India about 42000 government offices have been linked to this **GeM** website. Hence the opportunities for sale across India has been given. **GeM** operates as an easy way for the government to procure products via e commerce which has been discovered by the modern world. And MSMEs like us it is a good opportunity for doing direct sales with the government. Now it is a permanent opportunity.

**MSMEs** can register themselves as sellers using their UAN, Organization registration No, PAN, and Bank AC No.

**For Startups** if you have a telephone number with the **DIPP No** you can start your account immediately.

Since there is a chance for **Proprietorship, Partnership, LLP, Private Limited, Public Limited, Trust and Society** to participate, direct producers can participate in direct auctions.

Hence tradesmen can and brokers cannot benefit from this site. If the product you are manufacturing is of the least price, (Least 1–L1) then you get the chance to sell. For start ups there is a separate login. An opportunity to introduce their latest products, and to understand the government offers has been given.

## Exhibitions

**Exhibitions are being** held every day in each city globally. It happens in small cities and villages etc. the exhibitions are taking placing displaying all the products at one place or each product is placed at separate places, as per the department, as per the city, as per the technology.

There are some permanent exhibitions in some cities. For that, there are separate websites.

For instance in Chennai we have the **Chennai trade center**, in Coimbatore, we have the **CODISSIA hall**, in Hyderabad there is **HITEX**, in Delhi we have the **Pragati Maidan**, likewise across the nation there are permanent exhibition centers. Some of them have been established via the Indian Trade Promotion Organization of the Indian Government. Even abroad, such organizations operate the exhibitions in the permanent centers.

For such permanent organizations and the separate exhibitions are having separate websites for each programs. If we register the business related information in the websites, there is a chance of their sharing the details of the prospective exhibition with you via email or telephone. Even if you forget they will without fail intimate you on all programs. But you alone can decide which the program that suits you. Your requirements is the market for your product. For car manufacturing exhibitions there is no point in just manufacturing. In a car exhibition, there is no point in a pickle manufacturer participating. When spare parts manufacturers participate in the car exhibition, it will benefit both the spare parts manufacturer and the car manufacturer. Hence to participate in an apropos exhibition, one needs to register in a apropos website for the program. Some social – family exhibitions, take place. We should not deem that there is no point in our attending them. You might not get the chance at establishing a shop there, you might have persons who offer you a low priced raw material. You might get a chance at offering them a service product.

**JITO (Jain International Trade Organization)** conducts the JITO UDAAN Exhibition. JITO UDAAN 2019 took place in the year 2009 for Jain Community. Whether or not we desire it, the groups in our nation are split as per caste. Hence the industry too is divided as per caste. By going there, many good opportunities may come up for the MSMEs. In Tamil Nadu, **TADBE (TAMILNADU ADIDRAVIDAR BUSINESS EXPO)** exhibition takes place once every two years. Here the **Adi Dravidar** Entrepreneurs can display their products and services in the exhibition. We get the opportunity to share our products and services with the entrepreneurs there. Raw materials can be sold or we can purchase the products at a lower price from them and sell it to others. For that exhibition one can find information at the http://www.tadbe.in/index.php. If you register your email and your telephone No in the website, they will maintain you in this regard.

All the above trade exhibitions are just examples. Further several lakhs of exhibitions are being conducted. Globally many industrial exhibitions, as relates to industry types, and divisions, relating to family business are taking place. We need to understand as to in which exhibition should we participate.

## Putting Stalls in Exhibition

Are we going to establish a shop and project ourselves as sellers or are we going in as a visitor is something we need to decide. If we go as a visitor, we need to decide if we are going as buyers or as sellers which by itself will decide the sort of exhibition we are going to attend. Going in as visitors is free in most exhibitions. But if we were to establish a shop and sell, it is not free of cost. The rental for shop ranges from ₹ 5000–₹ 500000. Even a three day rental can go to several thousands or millions. It depends on the product that is displayed in the exhibition.

There is a difference between handloom and car exhibition. Hence the place, item and time decides the rental. As per the product the customers coming to the exhibition too will change. Even for handloom exhibitions the customers buying silk sarees are different from iron pressed cotton sarees. Depending on the customers, the rental differs.

Don't come to a decision that MSMEs cannot participate in the exhibitions. Our Indian Government, and state government helps us participate in the exhibitions in many ways. In any exhibition that takes place in India.

For the MSMEs to participate in that exhibition four times, and to exhibit their products or services, the government reimburses 80% of the shop rental in order to take a shop for rental in that exhibition. Even the commutation charges are paid.

If the business is in contact with Government organizations like NSIC, KVIC, MSMEDI and IC (International Cooperation), they get an authorisation letter for putting a stall in an exhibition, they create the opportunity for MSMEs like us to participate. Then they deposit the required amount with the exhibition coordinator. If these are overseas exhibitions, the government undertakes the air fare. Also it pays you 150 USD for three days for your expenses. To participate to the maximum extent in the exhibition and to exhibit your products and services is very easy. Not just exhibiting even marketing here is very easy. Hence anything is possible, exploit your opportunities immediately.

## Network Meeting

In the current times, Network meetings can enable several meetings in a day with various places. It is a very significant opportunity. During this meeting, the entrepreneurs, in a specific day, can meet at a specific place, share their information and give details of their industry. Each entrepreneur can share their ID and their brochure mutually.

Here many entrepreneurs participate from various areas. Hence contacts grow, and industry too grows. Many enterprises are operating to conduct such meetings. About Rs. 300 to Rs. 1000 is levied as the participation fees per day. With maximum participation, you will be able to attain new entrepreneurs and customers.

## Associations

**Industrial association is** an organization comprising various groups of industries. It is nothing new, it is the association mentioned by Buddha. The entrepreneur can join his organization with the association. But individuals cannot be members. Only industries can be members of this organization. Industrial heads can participate in the meetings or they can approve someone to represent the organization in the meeting. Here too network meetings can take place. When the business motives of the government is not conducive to us, approaching as individuals can be difficult.

But when we approach via such associations, circumstances conducive to us take place.

In our nation, there are associations functioning for more than 100 years. There are associations functioning for more than 50 years as well. There are many associations for large organizations, those for MSMEs, those for women etc. Associations for startups too have sprung up. There are associations for specific industries. For example, medical, and automobile industry are functioning. There are district based associations. We should join one of them deciding which one of them will help in exposing our products and services to the maximum number of persons. We need to look into our benefit and industrial benefit and take a decision on which association to join. Each association charges an annual fees for joining. When paying the annual fees, we need to be concerned if we are going to get a benefit worth the annual fees and then join. Annual fees is the operational fees of the association. The fees is decided depending on the information to be conveyed to you, to conduct meetings, to conduct seminars, to create information booklets containing member information, and based on the expenses incurred.

Just as they take decisions based on their needs, you too need to decide based on your needs. But right or wrong you need to function by joining an association. Industrial associations are important for contacting the government and procuring information immediately, to participate in network meetings, to know the opportunities in various districts, to participate in exhibitions, to get the government benefits, to participate in industrial classes, and to avail various other benefits. Join an association that is close to your industrial office, and something you can contact easily.

## Digital Marketing

Digital marketing is a method of marketing that is easy, that can help you get customer information, and to reach out to customers in an easy, cost effective and simple manner. There are many divisions like SMS Marketing, Mobile Phone marketing, Email Marketing, Search Engine marketing, and Social Media Marketing etc.

## SMS Marketing

**SMS Marketing though is an old method,** one needs to consider that 40% or majority of the persons don't carry a mobile with web facilities.

The rest have internet facilities. Totally there are about 80 crore cell phones in India. Most marketing agencies sell the cell phone numbers as classified information package. The Cell phone numbers are classified as sets based on persons receiving monthly salary, persons with loan card, working women, students, industrialists, doctors, engineers etc. you can send SMS of about 160 letters of necessary information, thus advertising your products and services by duly researching the sort of information to be sent to each category of persons.

You can send SMS in terms of new shop openings, festival greetings, and various other methods. You can use your website address in the SMS and directly invite your customers to your website and using the 160 lettered SMS, using this SMS way of marketing is best.

## Mobile Marketing

Mostly it is operated via **smart phones**. It is a marketing using the information they use. By the way of advertising on the screen of smart phones.

This marketing is carried out. It happens via the apps of the smart phone users.

## Email Marketing

Though it is a bit old method, it is regarded as one that directly reaches out to the customer. They way an SMS marketing functions, the same can be attained via email marketing and it can done even further. Just like cell phone numbers, the email addresses too have been categorized. By that the information that needs to reach the customer directly is sent to him directly. One can send images, videos, newsletters and greetings. By email you can get the customer to directly visit your website.

## Search Engine Marketing

Search engine marketing is mostly based on the google.com search engine. But there are other search engines.

This marketing method, is designed based on the key words used to search by the customers in the search engine. If the customer searches for tailors in

Chennai, and if you have advertised as a tailor, for the customer who searches for the tailors required, it has been designed in a way that your advertisement can be found. A separate fees is levied for advertising and another fees for the customer to click the advertisement. To make the customer register in your website, there is a separate fee levied. When the search engine searches for key words, in order for your advertisement to be shown over the website of your competitors, to prioritize the viewing of your website, we need to reserve those key words for us by paying a fees. There is a increase in fees for clicking based on key words.

## Social Media Marketing

The development of the internet, has made the globe to a single city, and has brought people closer. For this the social media has contributed a lot. Facebook, Twitter, LinkedIn, WhatsApp and Instagram, are the various available social media. People spend a lot of time on social media. They convey their desires to the world.

They share photos, videos, they openly share information on the preferred food, about the favorite actors, and the political opinions. Each individual has his individual wishes. Most persons are coordinated using such desires. The details on education, job, designation that they convey indicate their social and financial state. For this the social media is helpful in conveying the advertisement directly to individuals.

The social media that integrates friends, based on the political happenings, daily happenings, and individual information, the social media that merely helps register images, the social media that integrates industrialists, based on their industry and skills, people are thus integrated based on the social media. The place where people are integrated is for us the market. Hence realize where the customers that are ready to buy your products or services are located, advertising in that social media will help you.

Not just social media, concerning all methods of digital marketing, we need to decide which is required by us.

Though we can perform all of this by learning it ourselves, since the entrepreneurs keep getting other works, a good digital marketing agency has to be selected, and it is my opinion that it has to be delegated to them and we should supervise the same.

The way you are a specialist in your field, digital marketing is a profession, it has currently helped developed MSMEs. The person who is into that field too must be an expert. They will know the latest developments and the current technology.

By the experience gained by advertising to people earlier, we can display a good experience in our advertisement without any errors. Sometimes they may counsel you on the apropos media for your product. Select a good agency and delegate your digital marketing work to them. Apportion a part of the costs towards monthly digital marketing expense.

## Export Marketing

When the local market cannot be grasped by us, I can hear you saying, is exports practicable for MSMEs. But the reality is not such. Out of the Indian Exports about 40% of it is done via the MSME. In this India has currently done 292 billion dollars of exports and has gained the 19th position in the world.

China which has done about 2792 billion dollars of exports is in the first place. Our contribution to the global exports is only 2%. If our MSMEs were to contribute to the exports there are growth opportunities for us. The contribution of china which is in the first place is about 13%. The gap between the first place and us is about 11%. Hence we have a lot of opportunities. Hence it is clear the MSMEs have lots of opportunities.

About 16000 goods are being exported from India. Of which 600 are produced by MSMEs. When the global contribution of MSMEs to exports is nearly 95%, our MSME contribution to exports is a mere 40%. The 6000 products exported by the MSMEs is nearly 100 million dollars. Hence exports is not impossible. Ok let me discuss exports and imports in detail later. Here let us see marketing export alone.

There are 32 councils established by the Indian government to incentivize exports.

After you verify as to which council your product comes under, you should become a council member. Via that you will gain information on exports and your products. You will get the opportunity to exhibit your products in overseas exhibitions. There will be export training classes by this you gain information immediately.

For some products, the government gives an incentive of about 5% to do exports. That is if you export, the government gives you money. It is not merely the profits given by the customers, the government too gives you money. It is a dual profit. Further for exports local taxes are not applicable. That is there is no tax. Should we lose such an option?

Further exports is not like the local market where you sell each product to your customers and make profits. Once you get a customer in the exports, you can live to the fullest. For all export orders, are a total business. They are not retail business. But getting a customer and gaining his trust are challenging tasks.

That is why you need to be a council member related to that product. Then you can gain their trust.

Generally for all products **FIEO – Federation of Import Export Organization** which is an Indian government organization, invites customers, and arranges customers meeting.

They offer a 6 month training and diploma in exports and imports, hence you need to be a member of FIEO, and get the approval for exports of all kinds of products. Then in order to increase exports, you need to be a member of the council which you require or something that fits your product.

The Indian MSME Ministry runs the website called the www.msmemart.com. In this website if you as an industrialist were to directly share your business information, there is a chance of your directly contacting the customers. The tenders of many overseas governments too comes up in that website. It is of note that the www.msmemart.com is operating for the export growth of MSMEs.

# Chapter 6

# Start-Up

Are all fresh enterprises start up enterprises? Most of the unemployed engineers in India introduce themselves as a startup entrepreneur. Some entrepreneurs classify themselves as startups based on the new enterprise they have commenced. But they are not start up enterprises.

As of 2013, in nations like America, some regulatory bodies were commenced for startups. In the year 2016 in India, the mottos of startups were formulated. On January 11, 2011 the action plan for the same was formulated. In order for startups to benefit from the Indian schemes, the Indian government has defined the industrial organizations.

## Definition

When a new product or service is upgraded and created with a business intent, or if there is a new modification to the process for creating a product or service which has been previously inexistent, such an enterprise is called as a startup.

The product or service or its procedure of a startup should lend a value addition to the customer or should lend a value addition to his work flow.

Definitely that enterprise, should be registered as per the Indian Organization Act 2013 a **Private Ltd** concern, or as per the Indian Partnership Organization Act 1932 a **Partnership** Concern, or as per the defined Indian Liability Partnership Organization Act 2008, a **Limited Liability Partnership** concern.

An enterprise is considered as a startup for 10 years from the date of registration. The organization which has been registered under the above Acts should also be registered with the **Department of Industry Policy and Promotion**. When you register here, the **DIPP** after registration gives you a **DIPP Number**. If that Number is given, it implies that your enterprise has been authorized by the Indian Government. But the above rules are entirely to avail the government schemes only.

But it is my opinion that the startups don't come under a definition. The startups without definition, will use their free thinking, come up with fresh thoughts.

But when the government creates a scheme, it cannot do so for each organization separately. Hence the government has framed such definitions that benefit each and every Start-ups.

But there are lots of opportunities spread out globally. They cannot be measured. If you don't wish to avail the Indian Government's offers, you don't need to follow the above procedures. But to get the government's offers you need to follow the above procedures. Let us see each of the offers of the government below.

1. **Income Tax exemption for the first three years.**

2. **The startups can participate in all tenders of the government from the date of commencing.**

3. **You can sell directly in your name in the website www.gem.gov.in and You can decide the price. You can also change it. Opportunity is given to start a new industry by analyzing the administrative confusions in the industry.**

4. **Pre Experience and qualification is not required for tenders.**

5. **You can register in DIPP and get a DIPP number without any Goods and Services Tax certificate (GST).**

6. **Concession on Fee s are offered for Startups to register the protection, logo, and business seal, of your findings in the Intellectual property rights department.**

7. **The Application of IPR for protection rights, are sent for fast track service and it has been ordered that a speedy decision has to be taken.**

8. To fill the petitions for intellectual property rights, team of helpers have been appointed

9. In the starting stages to avoid the red tape situation, in order for the organizations to self-certify, six Labor Welfare rules and three Environmental Acts have been amended for startup friendly.

10. By creating the website http://startupindia. gov.in start-ups, mentors, incubators, investors, entrepreneurs and organizations helping in government departments, each have been offered a separate facility, and a conducive environment has been created for them to function under a single umbrella.

11. Separate Policies have been created for the startups in each of the 29 states and various UTs, and in order for the state governments to help the startups, a conducive situation has been created.

12. Using a ₹ 10 K crores Venture capital fund, facility has been created to invest the corpus fund via the SIDBI

13. A simple exit policy has been created and has been changed over to 90 days for the Startups under the Insolvency and Bankruptcy Code, 2016

14. **The old schemes that were functional via about 40 government organizations, new schemes have been designed for startups.**

## Innovation and Value Addition

The English term startup is not translated to as new organization. If someone read this newly they would find in manner. But I would translate it only as an Innovative Startup organization. All organizations that are newly found are will be deemed as a Startups generally.

But what actually happens in the case of startup companies is, by an organization starting, it is not considered a newly found organization. Rather only an organization that contains innovative aspects is called startup organization. Hence if there is no innovation in an organization, it is not deemed as a startup organization.

Innovation here refers to the novelty in your products or there should be something novel in the product development procedure. If in case your organization is service based, your service has to be new.

Another issue we need to understand using that definition is, innovation implies value addition to someone's life. Since the cell phone has a camera and one can take and send photos immediately, it prevents carrying a photographic camera with us at all times and it also reduces the burden of carrying a photographic camera, and this is value addition to someone's life. That value addition is beneficial to him.

## Value Addition

**Value addition,** also implies something else. This has to be understood by the entrepreneurs clearly. When a person buys and sells a product, if there is value addition, there will also be a price increase.

That is when you buy and sell rice, it has lesser value than when you buy rice and made as flour and sells the flour. The same flour when sold as Dosa and idly, you get more price, i.e a product when subject to an addition process, leads to value addition.

**Another example**, when iron ore is bought and sold, it has lesser value that when made as the iron rod and sold. If a long rod is cut and bent as a square or circle as required in construction, you get further more price. Here one needs to observe the value addition not the innovation.

Nothing is a new product, nor is it a new finding. When thinking during business startup, as to the choice of product, one needs to think about this as well. Since most are confusing with innovations and value additions, we had to discuss this here. What we need to understand from the above examples is, if there is value addition to a product, it implies a process. Flour is ground and rod is bent. It implies a process. Direct sales leads to less profits and increases brokers. This reduced by value addition. This is the significance of value addition.

## Incubator

Another aspect of the startup is the incubator. Incubator is place or environment which facilities, startups to formulate their ideas in to Product, the innovations that are not complete are made to grow, and made complete and makes it to profitable business. Incubators can be both governmental and private. Whatever it may be, it is meant for growth of organizations. Operating an incubator is deemed to be a business in itself by some organizations. There would be given development training, entrepreneur training, office training, and offers services like a place for running a business.

In order to give industrial counselling, an industrial counsel team is set up, and counselling is offered as a fee for service. If one were to register under www. startupindia.com the government offers these as free service. But private organizations charge a fees for the same and are doing it as a separate business in itself.

Regarding India, it was only in the year 2016, the government rendered a separate attention for the startup industry.

The startup industry has attained recent attention to the extent of government interference. But since the private organizations were into this even earlier, they have some advantages.

If the government does not interfere in a very large country like India, a decent proceeding will not be possible. The government as a good work, established the startupindia.com, has brought all services under the same umbrella, and is working efficiently. Not just that many government departments have started separate incubators. All of these is unified under http://startupindia.com. Via the above website, there is facility for going into the website of these individual departments. Even financing institutes have been linked to this website, Venture capital Investors, Angel investors and all the financial institutes have been linked together.

Most financial institutes are not interested in financing startups. When most MSMEs itself face challenges approaching banks for financing, the startups that have no plans or thoughts in place face lots of difficulties. The only opportunity they have is Venture capital Investors and Angel investors.

Some large institutions are interested in financing the startups. They too guide the startups using incubators.

The government using a ₹ 10000 crore venture capital fund, via the SIDBI Bank has been monitoring it. In the future, I expect it to get a full form. These should be noted by the MSMEs.

A small Idea can take you suddenly to heights. The advantage of startups is when starting they are all MSMEs. But when the correct opportunity presents itself, they have the chance of transforming suddenly into a larger enterprise. There are startups in India that have a turnover of ₹ 10K Crores within 10 years.

There are lots of opportunities, hence it is the duty of MSMEs to be aware of all the opportunities.

The Pitch fest which is a brain storming session run only for startups is something the MSMEs should participate too. There we might get lots of contacts. You too will get lots of new ideas.

## Chapter 7

# Export-Import or Interational Business

Most MSMEs think that Export-import or International business implies a business only for large organizations. That is very wrong. For in India about 45% of the exports is via the MSMEs. Our share of global exports is very less. India has a mere 2% share of global exports. Out of the 2%, 45% of the share belongs to MSMEs. Despite that, the export share of India globally is very less.

Hence we need to travel a long distance. So there are lots of opportunities all around. The **Forex** values of nation appreciates due to exports. You have heard of Forex and dollar reserves. It is linked to exports. It should not be construed as term befitting some large organization.

Regarding exports, our entire nation is to be deemed as a single shop. The country sells a product. Another nation purchases it. Understand it that way. The buyer country pays us money. The seller nation gets money. Similarly it is vice-versa for imports.

It is via this a nation's Forex and dollar reserves increases. The nations that are into higher exports have a higher dollar reserve. When we import, the cash in hand is reduced. Hence not just our nation, all nations promotes exports.

I will not say import is wrong. We need to import essential items that we don't have. Export and import are natural actions. For it has been happening for ages. The advantage of export is only 0% tax is imposed on exports rather it is tax free.

The import process definitely mandates government regulation. Essential requirement have a low tax, and a higher tax for products that disrupt internal production. Not just that, tax imposition has many reasons. It depends on the periodically contingent government circumstances and motto, decisions etc.

Regarding imports, you are going to buy and sell it to local. That business is contingent on the local business. At times there are products we buy from one Country and sell it to another Country. That is regarded only as exports. We need to meet our expenses from the money received from customers only.

Hence all costs are apportioned to the product price. Hence when buying from one nation and selling to another, it is joined to the export price.

Though we say we are selling from one nation to another, we can do so only via an individual or organization. Even the government cannot do so directly. The government starts and sells through an organization only. For instance Boilers are sold via **BHEL (Baharat Heavy Electricals Limited)**, carriages via the **ICF (Integral Coach Factory)** to various nations as exports.

## How to Start

First you need to have **PAN** for export business. Then you need a bank AC which can be a savings or current account. You can do export and import via that. But for an organization one can do business via current account only. I have mentioned this before. I recommend current account.

Then you need to apply at the www.dgft.gov.in website and they will immediately give you a IE CODE (Import Export Code), earlier it used to take nearly 15 days to get the IE code.

Then the bank needs to give an approval certificate. Currently the government has made the procedures rather simple to encourage the exports. Earlier the IE code and PAN were different. But currently the PAN is used as an IE CODE. For this you need to register with the www.dgft.gov.in compulsorily.

The IE CODE (Import Export Code) is a mere ID. It is not the correct license for overseas business. But most claim that by have an IE code they have a license. But it is not so. To encourage exports, the Indian government, has 32 Export Promotion Councils. Of which 14 of these councils operate under the Department of Commerce. Others function as separate units. If you register as a member in one of these units you will be given a **RCMC (Registration cum Membership Certificate)**, it functions as the license for exports. Ok let us see each of these export councils.

| SNO | NAME OF THE EXPORT PROMOTION COUNCILS | SUBJECT |
|-----|----------------------------------------|---------|
| 1 | Agricultural land processed food products export Development Authority (APEDA) | Farming and preserved food products |
| 2 | Apparel export Promotion Council | Garments, clothes |
| 3 | Basic Chemicals Cosmetics and Dyes export Promotion Council (CHEMEXCIL) | Simple chemicals |
| 4 | Carpet export Promotion Council | Carpets |
| 5 | Chemicals and allied products export Promotion Council (CAPEXIL) | chemicals and related chemicals |
| 6 | Coffee board | Coffee |
| 7 | Cashew export Promotion Council (CEPC) | Cashews |
| 8 | Coir Board | Coconut fiber |
| 9 | Council for leather | Leather |

| 10 | Engineering export Promotion Council (EEPC) | Engineering items and equipment |
|----|---------------------------------------------|---------------------------------|
| 11 | Export Promotion Council for handicrafts (EPCH) | Handicrafts |
| 12 | Gem and jewellery export Promotion Council | Gems and jewels |
| 13 | Handloom export Promotion Council (HEPC) | Handlooms |
| 14 | Indian oil Seeds under produce export Promotion Council (IOPEC) | Oil seeds and allied products |
| 15 | Indian Silk export Promotion Council (ISEPC) | Silk items |
| 16 | Jute product development export Promotion Council (JPDEPC) | Jute products |
| 17 | Marine Products export Development Authority (MPEDA) | Marine products |
| 18 | Pharmaceutical export Promotion Council (PHARMAEXIL) | Medicinal products |
| 19 | Rubber board | Rubber products |
| 20 | Power loom development export Promotion Council (PDEXCIL) | Power loom products |
| 21 | Projects export Promotion Council (PEPC) | Total construction and infrastructure items |

*Continued...*

| 22 | Service export Promotion Council (SEPC) | Service industry |
| --- | --- | --- |
| 23 | Shellac export Promotion Council (SEPC) | Forest items excluding trees |
| 24 | Spices Board | Masala products |
| 25 | Sports goods export Promotion Council (SHEFEXIL) | Sports products |
| 26 | The cotton textiles export Promotion Council (TEXPROCIL) | Cotton textiles |
| 27 | The plastics export Promotion Council (PEXCONCIL) | Plastic products |
| 28 | The Synthetic and Rayon Export Council (SRTEPC) | Synthetic fibers and allied products |
| 29 | Tea Board | Tea leaves products |
| 30 | Tobacco board | Tobacco products |
| 31 | Wool and woollen export Promotion Council (WWEPC) | Woolen textiles |

Each of the 31 councils are each meant for one segment of product and continue to operate individually. You need to find out the council under which your product comes and you should become a member of the same. Once you become a member, you get the certificate for the same. It is called the RCMC (Registration cum Membership Certificate. It implies that you have obtained the license for exports and imports.

It doesn't mean that you can export only the above products. About 16000 items are being exported. Of which 6000 belong to MSMEs. If it has to be mentioned here, I need to dedicate a separate book for the same. But they definitely come under one of the councils mentioned above. If not, there is a list of restricted items. Please verify that. There is a list of restricted countries as well. You cannot export to these countries.

Under EEPC there are hundreds of engineering industries. From Solar light panels to hammers everything comes under engineering department. Hence all of these are exported under the EEC.

Hair can be exported only under the PEPC or Plastic Export Promotion council. Hence research the council under which your product comes and you need to avail the membership.

## Customs House Agent

When it comes to export and import, each MSME, need to contact the CHA. Each exporter should be familiar with CHA like a family doctor. The work of the CHA he has to register the export or import business, and protect data of the same. The contact of a good CHA helps in continual business growth. From the time of getting an overseas sale order, to each and every transaction cannot transpire without his support. The CHA is appointed via government license, but the CHA is in touch with the organizations that send the goods. Not just that, insurance organizations too will be in touch with them. Further they know each and every goods transaction. They know the charges for each port and tonnage. Hence before we intimate our customers about pricing, it is best to consult the CHA.

## Insurance

The Indian government has started an insurance organization for export import business, and has been operating it for several years. It is called the ECGC Ltd. Or formerly Export Credit Guarantee Corporation Limited. It helps insure each transaction in overseas business. Hence the ECGC is the prior insurance to compensate the losses for the products you send, for the transport, and transactions. There are special insurances for MSMEs.

## Searching for the Customer

**Ok** what is next, you need to search for a customer. Where is your customer and in which country is he present – write down these. Write letters and mails overseas and find out a qualified customer who can procure and sell your goods. In the Indian embassies overseas Brochure exhibitions take place. You don't need to participate directly. It is enough that you send the Organization brochure. The Indian government is operating the website www.msmemart.com for exporting MSMEs only. Go into the website and register your organization. Via that there is a chance of getting many foreign government contracts.

Also register in the private websites like amazon. com, alibaba.com, you might get opportunities from any corner of the world.

## Sending Samples

The next level in exports is that once you get your customers, they will request samples. Then you have to send those. But left to me the export and import field is a place where anyone can at any time get duped.

We see so many cheatings in the Local business too. We would have seen many times a situation where we send the product but don't get the money. There are organizations that receive the money but don't send the goods. Hence the same issues can come up in overseas business too.

We cannot blindly trust that a white People will not cheat. Is it not? Be it anyone, get the advance money and then send your products. Let it be a low value product or low volume product, get an advance first and then send the products. If we keep giving the samples bit by bit, who will meet the other expenses?

There are many costs like costs of sending and product price etc. We may incur silent losses. When sending samples it is good to use a government organization like India Post. Most overseas customers trust the India Post. Hence they will trust you. For getting a small amount of money use the western union to do so. For this the charges are per kilo. For sending these small samples you don't need to go to the toll gate.

## Costing

**Just because,** the item is yours doesn't mean that you can increase the prices at your whims and fancies. Don't ask me "don't I know how to decide the price". Most MSMEs think that the overseas customers are not aware of the inland prices. That is where the MSME entrepreneurs go wrong.

If a customer asks a rate, what if we fix the rate at our whims and fancies. Then you won't get invited by him. Export sales is like a wholesale. It is not meant for individual sales.

They procure it from you and send it to the various shops in that country. When it goes from your customer to the shop, there will be a price increase. When it goes from the shop to an individual there will be another price hike. If in this situation you hike the price, it won't be conducive for their profits. Hence fix the price cautiously.

Also remember that your customer has been procuring this product from someone else all these years. He might search for another seller like you so that he can buy at a lower price. If you hike the price, will he not recognize it immediately? Hence decide to do a business at a low profit. More sale will get you more profits.

## FOB – Free on Board

**FOB Price is** the product price that is used to get your product to the sea port or airport. Hence some may ask you for such a price. For your customer may have goods transport carriers that he is familiar with. Hence since he uses them frequently, he will be aware of this transport costing.

## CIF (Cost, Insurance & Freight)

**CIF Price** is the cost of the goods reaching the sea port or airport, it includes the transport costs, insurance and product cost.

## C&F (Cost & Freight)

**C&F Price** implies, apart from the insurance for the goods reaching the sea port or airport, the total cost. My opinion is not to undertake any transport or transaction without insurance. If your customer asks you're the price ex insurance, you need to add that in to the product price.

You will be able to quote the price immediately if you are in touch with the CHA or the Logistics organization. If the decision is not taken on the date of price quotation, there is a chance they may come back after a month and seek the old rates. When asking for price, tell them it is up to a specific date.

# Chapter 8

# Access to Finance

Financial restrictions are present at all times for the MSME entrepreneur. When banks offer loans to MSMEs it is from a state of panic. MSMEs are depending on banks and governments. To get a loan from institutions apart from banks and to come out is a challenge for MSMEs. But the MSMEs contribution to our nation is despite the various challenges it faces.

The government realized the importance of MSMEs and in the year 2006 has offered many offers, discounts, etc for the MSMEs to its advantage. Many state governments offer their own offers, schemes and discounts etc. Further they are the agents for the federal government and help the MSMEs avail the benefits. We the MSMEs need to understand that no government offers loans. It merely offers schemes and discounts, only banks offer loans.

## SIDBI (Small Industries Development Bank)

**SIDBI (Small Industries Development Bank)** were established in 1990 and have been functioning since then for small industries growth. It offers direct and covert loans to the MSME entrepreneurs. I hope you understand the term direct. Covert implies offering loans via the other banks, State Finance Corporations, Non-Banking Finance Corporation, NABARD offers loans for agricultural and farming industry, and SIDBI offers loans for MSMEs. Many loan schemes of the central government such as MUDRA, Stand up India, Start up India are monitored by the government via SIDBI. The work of web development and monitoring is being done by SIDBI.

## UYEGP (Unemployed Youth Employment Generation Programme)

UYEGP (Unemployed Youth Employment generation programme, is a scheme created by the TN government. If the youths in TN are desirous of being self-employed without getting into a job, this scheme is with the aim of fostering a small level business. Loans from ₹1–₹10 lakhs is being offered via this scheme. The government gives back a grant of 25% for the industry you are into. About 10% of the capital investment has to be done by the entrepreneur. Only if you have a minimum education of 8th grade can you participate in this scheme. This scheme offers maximum of ₹ 10 lakhs for Manufacturing, ₹ 3 lakhs for service and ₹ 1 lakh for trade industry. Since people approach for loans without knowing the industry, it offers a free industrial training for about 7 days.

You can apply via the website https://msmeonline.tn.gov.in/uyegp/index.php.

## PMs Employment Generation Program – PMEGP

**Via the** union government of India, this scheme is functioning across India, via the district industrial centres. This scheme offers maximum of ₹ 25 lakhs for Manufacturing, ₹ 10 lakhs for service. In this scheme as well, the government gives back a grant of 25% for the industry you are into. About 10% of the capital investment has to be done by the entrepreneur. Only if you have a minimum education of 8$^{th}$ grade can you participate in this scheme. Hence for those into the starting stages of business, can use this scheme.

You can apply via the below website. https://www.kviconline.gov.in/pmegpeportal/ pmegphome/index.jsp.

In this scheme, you will be given entrepreneur training from 6–10 days.

## NEEDS (New Entrepreneur cum Enterprise Development Scheme)

NEEDS – New Entrepreneur cum Enterprise Development Scheme, is run by the TN government. It is a scheme meant for offering loans up to

₹ 5 crores. It is a scheme created specifically for the first generation entrepreneur. You can participate in this scheme if you are qualified as a graduate, post graduate, ITI and industrial training via approved organization. Via this scheme about 25% grant or ₹ 30 lakhs whichever is less is being offered. You can apply via the https://www.msmeonline.tn.gov.in/needs/index.php. The TN government repays about 3% of the interest. Further it offers one month of free entrepreneurial training.

## CGTMSE (Credit Guarantee Scheme for Micro and Small Enterprises)

In CGTMSE (Credit Guarantee Scheme for Micro and Small Enterprises), loans are offered via the guaranteed funding trust created by the MSME industrial Ministry, and MSME development Bank jointly, the Indian government and the **SIDBI bank** have jointly and created a block fund of ₹ 6914 Crores, and continue to run this insurance scheme. This scheme has been designed that in the event that a MSME entrepreneur is unable to repay the loan, the same can be returned so via this scheme.

When a loan is availed earlier for that, from the entrepreneur about 1 to 1.85% of amount is levied as an insurance deposit. From the loan availed, about 50–85% loan guarantee is offered. In the pending 50% about 15% is availed as a promoter contribution.

In this loan scheme, maximum of about ₹ 2 Crore rupees is offered as a loan, under this scheme about 116 financial institutions have been grouped. Of this 18 of the nonbanking financial institutions. When the government comes forward to offer guarantee to the MSMEs, the banks get a confidence. In the past 15 years, the one crore loans that have been offered have been done so via this scheme. In the past financial year 2016–17, ₹ 1 crore loans have increased to ₹ 2 crore loans.

## 2% Interest Grant Scheme

Out of the loan interest obtained in year 2018–19, 2019–20, and the interest availed later for the outstanding loans, this is a scheme where the government offers back the 2% of interest. You can avail the benefit of this scheme if you have the correct GSTN, UAN.

## Stand-Up India Scheme

**Stand-Up India Scheme** is a special scheme operated specially for the scheduled castes, scheduled tribes, and the women of all groups. This scheme which is spread across India has been designed consisting of 125000 bank branches, and offering loans of ₹10 lakhs to ₹ 1 crore for each SC or ST community and a woman (the woman can belong to any community). It has been defined that the time period of loan repayment is 7 years. Under this scheme each bank branch has to offer loans to 2 persons. But the right of final decision has been given only to the bank manager. Like CGSTME, SIDBI and NABARD have unified have created a group fund of ₹ 5800 and created an organization called the Credit Guarantee Trustee Organization (NCGTC), and via the Credit Guarantee for Stand-up India Scheme (CGFSI) scheme, offers collaterals. In this scheme about 75% guarantee is being offered.

This scheme is offered only for green field business, why? Green field business? Are you scared? It implies a new business meaning one cannot avail a loan under this scheme for preexisting business. You can know more about this scheme from the website www.standupmitra.in. You can also apply via this website. You can select 3 bank branches near the center of your business when applying. You will definitely get a call from banks within 3 days. Since the scheme functions under the financial ministry, the banks directly reach the office address you had given. Hence apply with all information. None should be refused loans under this scheme. If there is a situation of refusal, there needs to be an explanation offered via a letter.

If someone is refused due to lack of training, he should be given sufficient training and given a loan. In the website www.standupmitra.in there are

500 training institutes, and the details of training. You can avail training via that and continue with your application. If you need a mentor, you can select one during application. I too am a mentor and my name is in the list of mentors. The additional information is that action has to be taken within 15 days of your application. This ensures that a promoter doesn't need to go back and forth without any purpose.

## PMMY MUDRA

This scheme has been designed in a way so as to integrate the would be business persons and preexisting business persons, it integrates all business sections like Manufacturing, service and retail. Under this scheme loans from ₹ 50000 to ₹ 10 lakhs are offered. Though it is named the Prime minister MUDRA scheme, Micro Units Development and refinance Agency (MUDRA) has been created to verify the growth of MSMEs.

In most MSMEs only 4% of persons got a bank loan. 96% used to conduct business taking a loan for a usury interest or a high rate of interest. This scheme is for eliminating them and to protect the MSME entrepreneurs. In this scheme, when we are repaying our loans, it is sufficient to pay the interest for the outstanding loan amount. This implies that this scheme eliminates the loan torture, and is meant to protect the MSMEs.

This scheme has been split into three types. It is designed as a child, teen and adult. The child loan (Sishu) is up to ₹ 50000, the teen loan (Tharun) is up to ₹ 5 lakhs and the adult loan ( Kishore) up to ₹ 10 lakhs. Another happy news is that no collaterals are required for this special scheme from Prime minister. To get this loan, you need to directly contact the bank branch. The banks are most welcoming for this. It is of pride to note, that in our nation, TN State has obtained the maximum loans and has repaid them.

## IFCI Ltd

The IFIC Ltd was established in 1948 to monitor and ensure the operations of the Indian government's industrial growth schemes, it is a non-banking financial institution. Most NBFCs, are private organizations. But this IFCI is a government body.

One cannot run any business with bank loans alone. Banks offer loans and help in business commencement, for Modules with project models, industries that are deemed to be stable, industries that believe that the procedures will be successful, and industries that are within their range. New industries and new ideas will not breed trust. For they are not verified.

If there be a failure the bank manager ends up being responsible. With due foresight out ancestors have as far back in 1948 created such a council.

Though there are more than ₹ 15 lakh schemes, it is my humble opinion that it is best to contact here for more than ₹ 1 crore schemes. Rather large schemes, new schemes, renewed schemes, etc should be contacted here. Here the officers are ready to capitalize such plans. Once you grow a bit, grow your confidence, and with due foresight contact this place with your plans. Enter this place with the due confidence that you have obtained all the features of an entrepreneur. I personally know many persons who have obtained funding via IFCI.

Earlier it was not easy to get an IFCI loan unless you are owning a private Ltd Organization. Currently it has been organized in a way that it is easy to get a loan of the minimum of ₹ 15 lakhs, further even if you are a sole proprietorship Organization, they can be contacted. It has been redesigned to support the MSMEs.

## Infrastructure Subcidy

### CLCSS (Credit Linked Capital Subsidy Scheme)

CLCSS (Credit Linked capital Subsidy Scheme) has been created for technology upgradation of pre-existing industries. ₹ 15 lakhs or 15% whichever is less is returned back where the investment has been made for purchase of equipment for upgrading the Production or product value. If you inform the bank manager of the crediting bank, he will apply and get you the due subsidies. Since you are getting the subsidies before the loan, the bank officials welcome this scheme.

## SFURTI (Scheme of Fund for Regeneration of Traditional Industries)

SFURTI (Scheme of fund for regeneration of Traditional Industries is something for safeguarding the tradition industries and the handicraft industries are clustered and they are protected and made to last for long. Any tradition industry employing a similar work but with various handicrafts person can use this scheme. Mat, jewels, traditional lamps and lock manufacturers can use this scheme.

We are aware that each aspect of India is related to a product. For several years the industries had been operating under the kings regimes. At that time there was a group of persons in an industry for each place.

One can avail aid from ₹ 2.5 crores to ₹ 5 crores in this scheme. For an industrial cluster with 500 handicrafts persons or lesser, the amount is ₹ 2.5 crores, for those industrial clusters with greater than 500 workers, can avail ₹ 5 crores.

The cost for creation of plans, for unifying the handicrafts persons, for conducting meetings, one can avail 10% or ₹ 25 lakhs whichever is less in this scheme.

You can apply in all the MSME development Institutes, those coming under one or two revenue circles also can apply. Both circles can be adjoining districts.

## MSE-CDP (Micro Small Enterprises Cluster Development Programme)

MSE-CDP (Micro Small Enterprises cluster development Programme) is a scheme where the various MSMEs as a different aspects of in a similar industry are unified, and to establish a cluster of general use center, ₹20 crores are offered. Out of the ₹ 20 crores, ₹ 14 crores is offered as a government grant. You no need to return it back. If the industry cluster contains more than 50% MSME, Women's organization, SC/ ST organizations 90% rather 18 crores need not be returned back. To the extent of the project value, facilities have been made for land purchase at 25% cost. The industry cluster can avail the facilities of establishing an exhibition center, staff residence, street lights, solar panels, public equipment, and websites.

To establish a DPR, about ₹ 5 lakhs is offered. This scheme can be used for establishing first aid center, child care, restaurants, telephone center, databases, conference halls, drainage water purification center, raw materials godown, and many others.

A team of about 40 members can easily establish this. If all 40 are of Micro Enterprises, it is so good. A Private Ltd Organization can be created, and one can obtain funding for the same all the 40 persons in the Private Ltd should be appointed as a director.

The organization is called as (Special Purpose Vehicle ) SPV. That organization is going to run this scheme. To know more about this scheme you can contact the MSME development Center. You can contact me. At the state level, the SIDCO has been appointed as a supervisory body.

All of the above is government scheme. Left to me, rather than memorizing the government schemes, you need to design your business plan, and to think of growth of your plans. When you approach a bank to get a loan for your business plans, you should not discuss the government plans with the manager. Create a framework for your business plan, write it down, explain it to the manager, and prove to him that it is profitable.

If you can made the bank understand that your plan is going to be successful without discussing the government schemes, and subsidies, the banks will come forward and explain to you as to which plan will offer you subsidies. If the bank is ignorant despite this you can explain the plan and subsidies and its significance. But most banks are aware of this. For the bank staff continuously meet promoters like you.

Also they are in touch with the government.

Left to banks they think in terms of your financial success, with no technological hassles, and to be stable till the time period of loan repayment.

In this situation if you discuss the government subsidies and schemes, there is a chance of deciding that you have come to receive the grant and spend it. You need to create an impression on the bank manager that you are going to return the loan.

Without the banks MSMEs cannot grow. Hence your friendship with the bank is a must. Till we are in business, bank contacts are very important. A bank person will continue to be a bank person for a lifetime.

In the situation there is a chance that he may not give you a loan. But he may help your next scheme, if at the first trial, your bank loan is cancelled, you don't need to be angry. There is a chance the same bank person may help you again.

Further don't spend time thinking about banks alone, NBFCSs can be contacted.

Venture capitalists and Angel investors can come forward to help you. If your scheme is overtly profitable, many private organizations too can come forward to lend you loans.

Further don't think individually, think of the above mentioned industry clusters, unify the MSMEs, you can try for a loan. Via this, you can get a financing without loans, you can execute larger plans and larger efforts.

## Chapter 9

# Organizations That MSMES has to be in Touch with and Their Benefits

Whatever the aid offered by government in development of MSME and startups, It may not be a direct aid but via some organizations. Due to the wrong feeding about government organizations, many don't register their organizations. 95% of the MSMEs run their business without registration. The number of entrepreneurs in private information gathering organizations, and the number of entrepreneurs in government organizations should be unified, is like a comparing a mountain and molehill. There is a large difference between the registered GST and registered UAN.

The government keeps announcing various good schemes periodically for MSMEs and startups. It is important to keep in touch with the departmental organization. Further by keeping in constant touch with government organizations, there will be a correct accounting in the government, they can select the correct scheme, and will be helpful to the same.

In that way the government organizations that help the MSMEs, and the aid to be procured via this, are being registered to some extent under the following headings. I would request humbly whether you are a MSME or start up entrepreneur to visit each office and get to know them.

The difference I feel between the MSME and startups is both innovation and the maximum profits. But the starting hitches are the same for both. Hence it is very good to keep in touch with government organization at the onset.

## Indian Intellectual Property Rights

Indian Intellectual Property Rights, with the HO at Mumbai, help the specific entrepreneurs and others. It offers all services including logo, trade mark, patents, and geographical identification of your products.

Regarding the Intellectual Property Rights, what is vital, is who registers first. The website www.ipindia. nic.in registers all the Intellectual Property Rights.

Information about that is also being issued. You can register in that website or go directly to the office. All cities have a branch office. Here they help in not just the Indian rights but also the overseas intellectual rights. To get a reimbursement of the costs incurred the MSMEs can contact, www.my.msme.gov.in.

### Patent

Regarding the different products, designs you have created, if the industry feels there will be a change due to innovation, you can register. Most start-ups, have innovated the product or process and added value, they too can register. Via this we can demand a share of royalty or profits from the industrial department that arises out of the product that is created using your products.

## Copy Rights

If you have created a book or lesson that is repeatedly published, you can apply for copy rights. If your book or lesson is being published for sales every time.

When it is being registered and sold, you can obtain royalty each time. In the recent past the issue that transpired between the Maestro Ilayaraja and SP. Balasubramanian is due to copy rights. If a music is created it belongs to the composer and not the singer. When the singer sings the song for profits and business, he needs to pay Royalty to the musical composer. In the website **www.copyright.gov.in,** one can apply for copy rights. Else there is a separate office in Delhi for this. It functions under the Indian commerce department.

## Trade Marks

**You can** obtain trade marks by registering the Logo or unique name of your organization, the font used to write that name, and the unique business identification created for business. The names of Coca cola, Colgate, and Amazon are written with unique words and registered. Similarly your organizations name too has to be unique and can be registered when required.

Some fake organizations print a name like ours, and may end up selling products.

The Word M of MacDonald's or the imprint of Nike shoes come under this category. There is a case between Achi masala and Achi Apakadi. Though they have not copied their mutual names, if the name is not registered, at a later date there can be similar confusions. There is a huge case between Thalapakatu and Thalapakatti Briyani and the case was in favor of Thalapakatti. There are several such cases.

## Designs

**The design of a building, product, car etc are registered.** You may be aware of the issues between the Apple and Samsung phones.

## Geographical Identification (GI)

Products like Erode turmeric, Kanchi silk, Dindigul locks which are related to the place can register to get a Geographical Identification. Then the product fetches additional price. They may get more sale orders. Geographical Identification prevents legally the sale of a product with that name which is being manufactured elsewhere.

Each MSME should register in the above manner. You can get the cost refunded. You just need a proper UAN. You can apply to the website www.my.msme. gov.in and refund your money.

## MSME-Development Institute

Under the MSME development supervisor's office, there are MSME training centers that are functional. They offer training for new entrepreneurs, selecting a proper industry for them, selecting a proper scheme for them, further to offer them the property consultation are the activities of this organization.

Further they move closely with the trade unions, and organizations for the benefit of preexisting industries and understand them, they work in tandem with the Industrial departments of the state government, they create industry clusters, they procure the funding via the state government from the central government, they create opinion polls and awareness meeting for their required training, and upgrade their status.

### MSME Data Bank

The site www.msmedatabank.in has been created, the MSME information is gathered, and via that the key points are gathered, to create new schemes, they use this site. Hence if all the MSMEs were to register in this website, you will obtain MSME related information directly into the email under the direct government observation.

## National Awards

For MSME entrepreneurs who are operating nationally, awards are being offered year around. It is meant for encouraging, incentivizing, and to help the MSMEs. The Producers and service persons are separately given awards. Similarly MSMEs are given awards separately.

## CLCSS (Credit Linked Capital Subsidy Scheme)

For technological development via CLCSS (Credit Linked Capital Subsidy Scheme), apart from awarding 15% subsidy for the skill upgrading of MSMEs, it offers required training. By skill upgradation, the ordinary labour can be made to skilled labours and it makes them the staff of MSMEs or individual entrepreneurs.

## My MSME

The MY MSME App installed in the Android mobile helps in unifying all the MSME entrepreneurs and can get to know the services of the MSME Ministry, every week. You will get the MY MSME from the google play store of the Android phone.

## MSME Samadhan

The organization MSME Samadhan helps get the outstanding amounts for MSME. If an organization doesn't pay within 45 days for the product or service it has procured, as per the terms of the RBI, it has to pay three times the interest rate announced by the RBI and the principal. This strict measure has been implemented by the Union government to protect the MSMEs. Via this maximum amounts of money is being procured.

## Industry Clusters

It helps in discovering natural industrial clusters, creating of new industry clusters, and helping them procure the required finance. The details of Industry clusters have been made out in the previous title of availing of finances.

## Marketing Assistance

It offers the opportunity for each MSME to participate 4 times in the exhibition conducted nationally and twice in that conducted Internationally per year. The Vendor Development Programme is conjoined with Public works departments, and helps the MSME entrepreneurs interact directly with the Public works officials, and transforms the MSME entrepreneurs to vendors. Due to that the MSMEs get continuous opportunities from the government Public works organizations. Further at a divisional level, industrial exhibitions are held throughout the year, and there is a coordination between the MSMEs.

## NSIC (National Small Industries Corporation)

**The** NSIC (National Small Industries Corporation), was established in the year 1955 for helping the MSMEs. **It has** its head office in Delhi, and has 123 offices. For helping the software entrepreneurs, software parks are created of 53000 square feet in Delhi and and 48000 sqft in Chennai and helps each organization get about 400–4000 square feet of rental space at a low rate. Though it is a profit oriented organization, it has been helping the MSMEs for ages. It serves in all angles like raw materials purchase, to get equipment, to participate in exhibitions, to participate in lease, to help get marketing loans, to help procure subsidies. To know more about this keep in touch with www. nsic.co.in.

### Are NSIC and MSMEs Similar Organizations?

**The above questions is** something that most MSME entrepreneurs raise. MSME ministry, is a head organization for helping all the MSMEs. What are the branches and organizations underneath the same ministry? The schemes created by the MSME ministry cannot be utilized directly. It has to be operated under an organization. One such organization is the NSIC.

But the NSIC is a profit generating industry. It does profit oriented activities like software exports, procuring and selling of raw materials for MSMEs. MSME ministry is a government body that works on a profit motive. It helps grow the MSMEs, and helps job opportunities development.

## Schemes

It runs various schemes like Raw Material Assistance scheme, B2B platform, industrial protection center, single registration scheme, marketing development scheme, marketing aid scheme, etc.

## Raw Material Assistance Scheme

Raw Material Assistance scheme is to help reduce the funding issues of MSMEs. If it helps procure a bank guarantee via the banks, based on that guarantee, the raw materials are procured either locally or from overseas for the MSMEs by the NSIC. It has been designed such that we can get the money from the customer and return it within 180 days. This way, by not spending any money from our person, and not touching the working capital, we can run our industry with ease. For this a subsidy fees will be taken from the transaction fees. For payments that are delayed beyond 180 days a specific interest will be imposed.

## B2B Platform (www.msmemart.com)

I have written in detail about the section on overseas business concerning this platform. It is being operated by the NSIC. There are various facilities like local and overseas lease, Information system of local MSMEs, facility for receiving money via internet, separate email IDs, internet facility in various languages, etc. Some fees is levied from the members to operate the scheme. But no fees is levied for new members joining in, but it offers a little bit of facilities for them.

## NSIC Technological Service Center

Testing centres are established in NSIC technological service center, Skills development center, Hi-tech raw materials, raw materials testing center, have been established. Special facilities have been created for the Pump producers to test their pumps. By paying a small fees, we can make use of these test centers.

## Marketing Assistance Scheme

Via the Marketing Assistance Scheme, the NSIC helps in establishing shops at the overseas exhibitions. It offers the opportunity to participate 4 times in India and 2 times overseas in the annual exhibitions. In the days of participation it offers some amount of boarding and lodging costs as well. After you spend these there is a procedure for reimbursement.

## SPRS (Single Point Registration Scheme)

By registering in the SPRS – Single Point Registration Scheme, one can participate in events designated by the point of contract, without Tender document fee or EMD, in order to participate in contracts under the 2012, 25% reservations for MSMEs for the collection targets of the Public Departments, as described earlier.

To facilitate participation in the concluded points of contract, to participate in events of ₹ 5 lakhs in the event mentioned by the point of contract, certificates are being awarded to MSMEs. To get that certificate some private evaluation organizations have been established. They will test the 100% skill levels of our organization, and issue this certificate. For this a small fees is levied. In order to increase the certificate of ₹ 5 lakhs, if you further apply in the NSIC, they will again perform a testing and issue a certificate. By this you can participate in the events specified by the concluded points of contract.

**Vendor Development Programmes**

In the program called Vendor Development Programmes, to create maximum vendors, they create review meetings between the government public departments and the vendors frequently. Here you can directly clarify your doubts from the officials of the public departments. For this you need to be always in touch with the officials of the NSIC.

# KVIC

**This** organization that was created in the year 1957, to encourage farming, to help in local industry, to coordinate local industries, and to upgrade the local industries. It has its head office in Mumbai.

The 25% subsidy that is offered by the PMEGP is via this organization. Via the website www.kviconline. gov.in that is operated by them, you can get to know the programs they conduct. Further you can apply in the above website for getting the 25% subsidy that is offered by the PMEGP.

## District Industrial Center

**The** persons aspiring for MSMEs, startups, and those aspiring for creation of new industries need to catch hold of the district industrial center. India consists of various states, and UTs and is divided into more than 650 districts. These districts are supervised directly by the central government. This organization was created by the central government in the year 1978 to upgrade the industries in these districts, to create startups, to unify the entrepreneurs, to render the required help, to obtain loans, to help them get subsidies, and to help them in industrial related issues. All the state capitals have this organization. Though established by the central government, the state Governments industrials schemes are being implemented. Most loan schemes are being implemented. Entrepreneur meetings, and industrial training is being imparted.

Most of the loan and subsidy schemes are being offered via the District industrial centers. A meeting is held every month in the auspices of the district collector, and to disburse loans speedily is the work of the district industrial centers. Via this the respective industrial growth of the districts is being supervised. Whatever be the issues that the entrepreneur's faces, that first point of contact is the district industrial center. The manager of the district industrial center is in touch with the all the industrial assistance organizations.

## National Scheduled Caste and Scheduled Tribe Hub

National Scheduled Caste and Scheduled Tribe Hub was established in the year 2016 for helping the growth of industries run by the SC/ST. As per the guidance of the private profitable organization called the DICCI (Dalit Indian Chamber of Commerce and industry), this National Scheduled Caste and Scheduled Tribe Hub has been established. This operates under the consultancy of the Advisory head **Mr. Milind Kamble,** Founder Chairman, DICCI.

The aim of this organization is to know the SC/ST entrepreneurs across the nation, and to unify them and to further to render the required help.

This organization has been created with about ₹ 480 crores of Venture funding in the year 2016 and operates with new operational planning.

About 25% of the nation's population is SC/ST. one cannot exclude growth by excluding the 25% of population. With the concept that to improve the nation's growth one needs to focus on the growth of this sector too, the National Scheduled Caste and Scheduled Tribe Hub was made to function under the MSME ministry and NSIC.

By the NSSH operating under the NSIC, it has been designed like the NSIC schemes. There is excess of offers in this more than what the other sectors receive from the NSIC, and is being operated as a special scheme.

In the year 2012, 4% of reservation of the PPP was made for the SC/ST entrepreneurs and their organizations. The NSSH organization is operating fast in order to run this scheme, to get information on SC/ST entrepreneurs, and to unify them. Though the reservation is 4%, most of the SC/ST entrepreneurs cannot be identified, due to which this reservation cannot be filled. But to the efforts of NSSH there has been some development.

The NSSH organization undertakes the total expenses of participation in the inland and overseas exhibitions, to establish shops, and that of travel expenses.

In case of bank loans, the processing of fees of up to Rupees one lakh will be refunded. 50% of the registration fees for SC/ST MSMEs shall be refunded as members of the export centers. The cost of technology testing operated by the NSIC Technological Service centers will be refunded. Thus many such assistance is being offered. 51% of the shares is allotted to the SC/ST in order for the general MSME entrepreneurs to enjoy the benefits and you too can create an organization and participate as a shareholder.

## Chapter 10

# Key Addresses

## Micro, Small & Medium Enterprises Development Institutes (MSME-DI)

1.  MSME-DI,
    Indranagar, (Near ITI Play ground),
    PO-Kunjaban, Agartala 799006
    Ph: 0381-2352013/9742
    Fax: 0381-2356570
    dcdi-agartala@dcmsme.gov.in
    www.msmedi-agartala.nic.in

2.  MSME-DI,
    34, Industrial Estate, Nunhai, (U.P.),
    Agra 282006. UP,
    Ph: 0562-2280879
    Fax: 0562-2280882
    dcdi-agra@dcmsme.gov.in
    www.msmediagra.gov.in

3.  MSME-DI,
    Tadong Housing Colony, P.O. Tadong,
    Gangtok 737102. Sikkim,
    Ph: 03592-231262/880
    Fax: 03592-231262
    dcdi-gangtok@dcmsme.gov.in
    www.msmedigangtok.gov.in

4.  MSME-DI,
    Opp. Konkan Railway Station. (Kepem Road),
    P.O. Box 334, Margao 403601. Goa,
    Ph: 0832-2705092/93, 2725979
    Fax: 0832-2705094
    dcdi-goa@dcmsme.gov.in
    www.msmedigoa.gov.in

5.  MSME-DI,
    65/1, G.S.T. Road, Guindy, P.B. 3746,
    Chennai 600032. Tamilnadu,
    Ph: 044-22501011, 044-22501475, 044-22501785
    Fax: 044-22341014
    dcdi-chennai@dcmsme.gov.in
    www.msmedi-chennai.gov.in

6.  MSME-DI,
    Vikas Sadan, College Square,
    Cuttack 753003. Odisha,
    Ph: 0671-2548006/077/049
    Fax: 0671-2611958
    dcdi-cuttack@dcmsme.gov.in
    www.msmedicuttack.gov.in

7.  MSME-DI,
    Industrial Estate, Gokul Road,
    Hubli 580030. Karnataka,
    Ph: 0836-2332334/2330589/2335634
    Fax: 0836-2330389
    dcdi-hubli@dcmsme.gov.in
    www.msmedihubli.gov.in

8.  MSME-DI,
    C-17/18, Takyelpat Industrial Estate,
    Imphal 795001. Manipur,
    Ph: 0385-2449096/2449096
    dcdi-imphal@dcmsme.gov.in
    www.msme-diimphal.gov.in

9.  MSME-DI,
    Industrial Estate Bamuni Maidan,
    Guwahati 781021. Assam,
    Ph: 0361-2550052, 2550073
    Fax: 0361-2550298
    dcdi-guwahati@dcmsme.gov.in
    www.msmedi-guwa- hati.gov.in

10. MSME-DI,
    Kham Bungala Campus, Kaladungi Road,
    Haldwani 263139. Uttaranchal,
    Ph: 05946-228353
    Fax: 05946-221053
    dcdi-haldwani@dcmsme.gov.in
    www.msmedihaldwani.gov.in

11. MSME-DI,
    36, B/C, Gandhi Nagar,
    Jammu 180004. J&K,
    Ph: 0191-2431077
    Fax: 0191-2450035
    dcdi-jammu@dcmsme.gov.in
    www.msmedijammu.gov.in

12. MSME-DI,
    107, Industrial Estate, Kalpi Road,
    Kanpur 208012. UP,
    dcdi-kanpur@dcmsme.gov.in
    www.msmedikanpur.gov.in

13. MSME-DI,
    10, Industrial Estate, Polo Ground,
    Indore 452003. MP,
    Ph: 0731-2420723
    dcdi-indore@dcmsme.gov.in
    www.msmeindore.nic.in

14. MSME-DI,
    22, Godown, Industrial Estate, Jaipur 302006. Rajasthan,
    Ph: 0141-2212098/3099/0553
    Fax: 0141-2210553
    dcdi-jaipur@dcmsme.gov.in
    www.msmedijaipur.gov.in

15. MSME-DI,
    Kurla Andheri Road, Sakinaka,
    Mumbai 400072. Maharashtra,
    Ph: 91-22-28576090/3091/4305
    Fax: 91-22-28578092
    dcdi-mumbai@dcmsme.gov.in
    www.msmedimumbai.gov.in

16. MSME-DI,
    C- Block, C.G.O. Complex, Seminary Hill,
    Nagpur 440006. Maharashtra,
    Ph: 0712-2510352/0046
    Fax: 0712-2511985
    dcdi-nagpur@dcmsme.gov.in
    www.msmedinagpur.gov.in

17. MSME-DI,
    Industrial Development Colony, Near ITI,
    Kunjpura Road, Karnal 132001. Haryana,
    Ph: 0184-2230910
    Fax: 0184-2231862
    dcdi-karnal@dcmsme.gov.in
    www.msmedikarnal.gov.in

18. MSME-DI,
    111&112, B.T. Road,
    Kolkata 700035. W. Bengal,
    Ph: 033-25770595/598
    Fax: 033-25775531
    dcdi-kolkatta@dcmsme.gov.in
    www.sisikolkata.gov.in

19. MSME-DI,
    Industrial Area B, Ludhiana 141003. Punjab,
    Ph: 0161-2531733/735
    Fax: 0161-2533225
    dcdi-ludhiana@dcmsme.gov.in
    www.msmedildn.gov.in

20. MSME-DI,
    Kokar Industrial Estate,
    Ranchi 834001. Jharkhand,
    Ph: 0651-2546133/2546266
    Fax: 0651-2546235
    dcdi-ranchi@dcmsme.gov.in
    www.msmediranchi.nic.in

21. MSME-DI,
    Okhla Industrial Estate New Delhi 110020.
    Ph: 011-26847223, 26838118/269
    Fax: 011-26838016
    dcdi-ndelhi@dcmsme.gov.in
    www.msmedinewdelhi.gov.in

22. MSME-DI,
    Patliputra Industrial Estate,
    Patna 800013. Bihar,
    Ph: 0612-2262719, 0612-2262186, 0612-2262208
    Fax: 0612-2261677
    dcdi-patna@dcmsme.gov.in
    www.msmedipatna.gov.in

23. MSME-DI,
    Near Urkura Railway Station,
    Bhanpuri Industrial Area,
    Raipur (C.G) 493 221. Chhattisgarh,
    Ph: 0771-2562312
    Fax: 0771-2562719
    dcdi-raipur@dcmsme.gov.in
    www.msmediraipur.gov.in

24. MSME-DI,
    E-17/18, Industrial Estate, Naini, Allahabad 211009. U.P,
    Ph :0532-2697468/6810
    Fax :0532-2696809
    dcdi-allbad@dcmsme.gov.in
    www.msmediallahabad.gov.in

25. MSME-DI,
    CHAMBAGHAT, Solan 173213.
    Himachal Pradesh,
    Ph: 01792-230766
    Fax: 01792-230265
    dcdi-solan@dcmsme.gov.in
    www.msmedihimachal.nic.in

26. MSME-DI,
    Kanjany Road, Ayyanthole,
    Thrissur 680003. Kerala,
    Ph: 0487-2360216/686
    Fax: 0487-2360216
    dcdi-thrissur@dcmsme.gov.in
    www.msmedithrissur.gov.in

27. MSME-DI,
    Harsiddh Chamber, 4th Floor,
    Ashram Road, Ahmedabad 380014. Gujarat,
    Ph: 079-27540619, 079-27544248, 079-27543147
    dcdi-ahmbad@dcmsme.gov.in
    www.msmediahmedabad.gov.in

28. MSME-DI,
    Rajaji Nagar, Industrial Estate
    Bangalore 560044. Karnataka,
    Ph: 080-23151540/582/583
    Fax: 080-23144506
    dcdi-bang@dcmsme.gov.in
    www.msmedibangalore.gov.in

29. MSME-DI,
    Narsapur Cross Roads, Bala Nagar,
    Hyderabad 500037. Andhra Pradesh,
    Ph: 040-23078857
    Fax: 040-23078131/32/33
    dcdi-hyd@dcmsme.gov.in
    www.msmehyd.ap.nic.in

30. MSME-DI,
    Institute,Goshala Road,
    P.O. Ramna,
    Muzaffarpur 842002. Bihar,
    Ph: 0621-2282486
    Fax: 2284425
    dcdi-mzfpur@dcmsme.gov.in
    www.msmedimzfpur.bih.nic.in

# Branch MSME-DI

1.  Branch MSME-DI
    F-19-22,Block D Ida, Autonagar,
    Vishakhapatnam 530012.
    Ph: 0891-2517942
    brdcdi-vish@dcmsme.gov.in

2.  Branch MSME-DI
    Apidfc Building 'C' Sector,
    Itanagar 791111.
    0360-2291176
    brmsme.itan@gmail.com

3.  Branch MSME-DI
    Vip Road, Jungle Ghat, Post Box No.547,
    Portblair 744103.
    Ph: 03192-252308

4.   Branch MSME-DI Link Road Point,
     N.S.Avenue, Silchar 788006.
     03842-247649
     brdcdi-silc@dcmsme.gov.in

5.   Branch MSME-DI Darrang College Road,
     Tezpur 784001.
     03712-221084
     brdcdi-tezp@dcmsme.gov.in

6.   Branch MSME-DI Amalepatti,
     Diphu 782460.
     Karbi Anglong (dist),
     03761-272549
     brdcdi-diph@dcmsme.gov.in

7.   Branch MSME-DI Masat Industrial Estate,
     Silvassa 396230.
     0260-2640933, 2643103
     brdcdi-silv@dcmsme.gov.in

8.   Branch MSME-DI
     3rd Floor, Annexe Building Amruta (Jasani) Building Premises,
     Near Girnar Cinema MG Road,
     Rajkot 360001. 0281-2471045
     brdcdi-rajk@dcmsme.gov.in

9.   Branch MSME-DI
     ITI Campus, Hansi Road,
     Bhiwani 125021.
     01664-242236
     brdcdi-bhiw@dcmsme.gov.in

10.  Branch MSME-DI Industrial Estate Digiane,
     Jammu tawi 180010.

11.  Branch MSME-DI Katras Road,
     Matkuria, Dhanbad 826001.
     0326-2303769/380
     brdcdi-dhan@dcmsme.gov.in

12. Branch MSME-DI
    L-11, Indl.Estate, Yeyyadi, Mangalore 575008.
    0824-2217936/96
    brdcdi-mang@dcmsme.gov.in

13. Branch MSME-DI C-1 & 2, Industrial Estate
    S.K. Mill Road, Gulbarga 585102.
    Ph: 08472-420944
    brdcdi-gulb@dcmsme.gov.in

14. Branch MSME-DI
    7, Indl. Estate, Tansen Road, Gwalior 474004.
    Ph: 0751/2422590
    brdcdi-gwal@dcmsme.gov.in

15. Branch MSME-DI Udyog Vihar,
    Chorhatta, Rewa 486001.
    Ph: 07662/222448
    brdcdi-reva@dcmsme.gov.in

16. Branch MSME-DI
    32-33, Midc, Indl. Area, Chikal Thana,
    Aurangabad 431210.
    Ph: 0240-2485430
    Fax: 0240-2484204
    brdcdi-aura@dcmsme.gov.in

17. Branch MSME-DI Lower Lachimiere,
    Shilong 793001. 0364 2223349
    brdcdi-shil@dcmsme.gov.in

18. Branch MSME-DI Hawakhana, P.O. Tura,
    West-Garo Hills 794001. 003651-222569.
    brdcdi-tura@dcmsme.gov.in

19. Branch MSME-DI Upper Republic Road, Aizwal
    0389-2323448
    brdcdi-aizw@dcmsme.gov.in

20. Branch MSME-DI Industrial Estate,
Dimapur 795001. 03862-248552
brdcdi-dima@dcmsme.gov.in

21. Branch MSME-DI C-9,Indl.Estate,
Rourkela 769004.
Ph: 0661-2507492
brdcdi-rour@dcmsme.gov.in

22. Branch MSME-DI New Colony,
Rayagada 765004.
Ph: 06852-222268
brdcdi-raya@dcmsme.gov.in

23. Branch MSME-DI 386,
Patel Road, Ram Nagar,
Coimbatore 0422 2233956 (tele fax)
brdcdi-coim@dcmsme.gov.in

24. Branch MSME-DI
Plot no. 76, Cge Colony,
Trichender Road,
Tuticorin 628003.
0461-2375345

25. Branch MSME-DI Chandpur Industrial Estate,
Varanasi 221106.
Ph: 0542-2370621
brdcdi-vara@dcmsme.gov.in

26. Branch MSME-DI Station More,
P.O. Suri, Birbhum 731101.
Ph: 03462-2554402
brdcdi-birb@dcmsme.gov.in

27. Branch MSME-DI 3&4,Industrial Estate,
    Sevoke Road, Siliguri 734001.
    Ph: 0353/2542487
    brdcdi-sili@dcmsme.gov.in

28. Branch MSME-DI
    RA-39 (Ground Floor), Urvashi (Ph. 2),
    Bengal Ambuja, Tarashankar Sarani,
    City Centre, Durgapur 713216.
    Ph: 0343-2547129
    brdcdi-durg@dcmsme.gov.in

## MSME – DI Extension Centre (Balsahyog)

Asstt. Director- In Charge Extn. Centre (Balsahyog)
Opposite Haldiram L-Block,Outer Circle, Connaught Circus
O/o the Development Commissioner (MSME),
Govt. of India, Ministry of MSME, New Delhi 110001.
Tel: 011-23411950, 23414364

## MSME - Technology Centers

1. Managing Director,
   MSME-Technology Centre (Indo German Tool Room),
   P-31, MIDC, Chikalthana Indl. Area,
   Aurangabad 431006. (Maharashtra)
   Ph: 0240-2486832
   Fax: 0240-2484028
   gm@igtr-aur.org

2. General Manager
   MSME-Technology Centre (Indo German Tool Room) Plot-5003,
   Phase-IV, GIDC Vatva, Mehmedabad Road,
   Ahmedabad 382445. (Gujarat)
   Ph: 079-25840966
   Fax: 079-25841962
   gm@igtrahd.com

3. General Manager (I/c),
   MSME-Technology Centre (Indo German Tool Room) Plot
   No.291/B,
   302/A, Sector-E, Sanwer Road, Industrial Area,
   Indore 452015. (MP)
   Ph: 0731-4210704
   Fax: 0731-2720353
   patogm@igtr-indore.com

4. General Manager, MSME-Technology
   Centre (Central Tool Room) A-5, Focal Point,
   Ludhiana 141010. (Punjab)
   Ph: 0161-2670057
   Fax: 0161-2674746
   info@ctrludhiana.com

5. Principal Director (I/c),
   MSME-Technology Centre (Central Institute of Tool Design)
   A-1 to A-8 APIE, Balanagar,
   Hyderabad 500037. (Telangana)
   Ph: 040-23772748
   Fax: 040-23772658
   pd@citdindia.org

6.  General Manager,
    MSME-Technology Centre (Central Tool Room & Training
    Centre),
    Bonhooghly Indl. Area, Kolkata 700108. (W.B.)
    Ph: 033-25776350
    Fax: 033-25772494
    cttc@cal.vsnl.net.in,
    debdutta.guha@msmetoolroomkolkata.com

7.  Managing Director,
    MSME-Technology Centre (Central Tool Room & Training
    Centre),
    B-36,Chandaka Industrial Area,P.O. Patia,
    Bhubaneswar 751024. (Orissa)
    Ph: 0674-3011701
    Fax: 0674-3011750
    cttc@cttc.gov.in

8.  General Manager,
    MSME-Technology Centre (Indo Danish Tool Room)
    M-4 (Part) Phase-VI, Tata Kandra Road,
    Gamharia, Jamshedpur 832108. (Jharkhand)
    Ph: 0657-2201261/2
    Fax: 0657-2202723
    reach@idtrjamshedpur.com

9.  Project Manager,
    MSME-Technology Centre (Tool Room & Training Centre)
    Amingaon Industrial Area, North Guwahati Road, Amingaon,
    Guwahati 781031. (Assam)
    Ph: 0361- 2680907
    Fax: 0361-2681030
    trtcghy@hotmail.com

10.  Principal Director
     MSME-Technology Centre (Central Institute of Hand Tools)
     G.T. Road, Bye Pass,
     Opp. Shaheed Bhagat Singh Colony Jalandhar 144008.
     (Punjab)
     Ph: 0181-2290225
     Fax: 0181-2290457
     info@ciht.in

11.  Managing Director
     MSME-Technology Centre (Institute for Design of Electrical
     Measuring Instruments)
     Swatantryaveer Tatya Tope Marg, Chunabhatti, Sion,
     Mumbai 400022. (Maharashtra)
     Ph: 022-24050301/2
     Fax:022-24050016
     info@idemi.org svrasal@yahoo.com

12.  Principal Director
     MSME-Technology Centre (Electronics Service & Training
     Centre),
     Dhela Rd, Kaniya, Ramnagar, Dist. Nainital 244715.
     (Uttarakhand)
     Ph: 05947-252168
     Fax: 05947-251294
     pd_estc@yahoo.com

13.  Principal Director
     MSME-Technology Centre (Process and Product
     Development Centre),
     Foundry Nagar,
     Agra 282006. (U.P.)
     Ph: 0562-2344673
     Fax: 0562-2344381
     info@ppdcagra.in
     paselvam@gmail.com

14. Principal Director
MSME-Technology Centre
(Process cum Product Development   Centre),
Sports Goods Complex,Delhi Road, Meerut 250002. (U.P.)
Ph: 0121-2511779
Fax: 0121-2530444
info@ppdcmeerut.com
ppdcmeerut@yahoo.co.in

15. Director,
MSME-Technology Centre (Central Footwear Training Institute),
C – 41& 42, Site 'C',
Sikandra Road, Industrial Area, Agra 282007. (U.P.)
Ph: 0562-2642005
Fax: 0562-2280882
info@cftiagra.org.in
sanatansahoo27@gmail.com

16. Director
MSME-Technology Centre (Central Footwear Training Institute),
65/1, G.S.T. Road,
Guindy, Chennai 600032. (Tamilnadu)
Ph: 044-22501529
Fax: 044-22500876
chennaicfti@gmail.com,
cfti@cftichennai.in

17. Principal Director
MSME-Technology Centre (Fragrance & Flavour Development
Centre), Industrial Estate, GT Road,
P.O. Makrand Nagar, Kannauj 209726. (U.P.)
Ph: 05694-234791
Fax: 05694-235242
ffdcknj@gmail.com,
shaktiffdc@gmail.com

18. Principal Director
    MSME-Technology Centre
    (Centre for the Development of Glass Industry),
    A-1/1, Industrial Area, Jalesar Road, P.O. Muiddinpur,
    Firozabad 283203. (U.P.)
    Ph: 05612-203238
    Fax: 05612-233087
    cdgifzbd@gmail.com

# Enterprise Facilitation Centres (EFC) of MSME-DI

1. EFC, MSME-DI (Branch), F-19-22, D Block, IDA,
   Autonagar, Visakhapatnam, Andhra Pradesh 530012.
   Ph.No. 0891-2517942/2701061
   srinu.appikonda@ dcmsme.gov.in,
   asrinu1981@ yahoo.in

2. EFC, MSME-DI,
   Patliputra Industrial Estate, Patna 800013. Bihar,
   naveenmsme1970@gmail. com

3. EFC, MSME-DI,
   Goshala Road PO Ramna, Muzaffarpur,
   Bihar 842002.
   kpsingh561964@gmail.com

4. EFC, MSME-DI, Raipur Near Urkura Railway Station,
   Bhanpuri Industrial Area, Birgaon 493221. (Chhattisgarh)
   gajbhiye95@gmail.com

# Enterprise Facilitation Centres (EFC) of MSME-DI

5.  EFC, MSME-DI, Shaheed Captain Gaur Marg, Okhla,
    New Delhi 110020.
    bpsingh10ke@gmail.com

6.  EFC, Extension Centre, New Delhi, C/o Extn.
    Centrte (Bal Sahyog) Opposite Haldiram
    L-Block, Outer Circle, Connaught Circus, New Delhi 110001.
    (Jointly by DI & PPDC)
    vikas.msmetdc@gmail.com

7.  EFC, MSME-DI,
    Opposite Konkan Railway Station, Quepem Road,
    Margao, Goa 403601.
    Deepa.gl@gov.in

8.  EFC, MSME-DI, Govt. of India,
    4th Floor, Harsidhh Chambers,
    Income Tax Circle, Nr. ESIC Office,
    ashram road, Ahmedabad,
    Pin 380014. (Gujarat)

9.  EFC, 3rd floor, Annexe Building,
    Amruta (Jasani) building Premises, Near Girnar Cinema,
    M.G. Road, Rajkot 360001. (Gujarat)
    (Jointly setup by DI & PPDC)
    Brdcdi-rajk@dcmsme.gov.in
    Prj.msmetdc@gmail.com

10. EFC, Branch MSME-DI,ITI Campus,
    Hansi Road, Bhiwani 127021. Haryana
    harpl2126@gmail.com

11. EFC, MSME-DI, Chambaghat, Solan 173213.
    Himachal Pradesh
    vsmsme@rediffmail.com

12. EFC, MSME-DI,
    Industrial Estate, Digiana,
    Jammu 180010.
    (Jointly setup by DI & PPDC)
    miraltafahmad2010@gmail.com

13. EFC, Room No-3,
    MSME-DI Ranchi, Industrial Estate, Kokar,
    Ranchi 834001. Jharkhand,
    neetu.msme@gov.in

14. EFC, Room No-8, Branch MSME-DI,
    Dhanbad, Katras Road, Matkuria,
    Dhanbad 826001.
    Jharkhand, skumar.msme@gov.in

15. EFC, Branch. MSME-DI, Masat Industrial Estate,
    Silvasa, UT, Dadra & Nagar Haveli 396230.
    Phone: 0260-2643103,
    Fax: 0260-2640933
    Solanki.pn@gov.in;
    brdcdi-silv@ dcmsme@gov.in

16. EFC, MSME-DI, Industrial Development
    Colony, Near ITI,
    Kunjpura Road Karnal 132001. (Haryana)
    tripathi.rachna8@gmail.com

17. EFC, Branch MSME-DI, Gokul Road,
    opposite to Gokul Garden,
    Hubli 580030.
    srcrasta@dcmsme.gov.in

18. EFC, Branch MSME-DI, M/o MSME,
    Govt. of India, C1 & C2, Industrial Estate,
    M.S.K. Mill Road,
    Kalaburagi (Gulbarga) 585102. Karnataka
    chatla.snmurthy@gmail.com

19. EFC, MSME-DI, Kanjani Road,
    Ayyanthole, Thrissur, Pin 680003.
    sindhumaniam@gmail.com

20. EFC, MSME-Development Nucleus Cell,
    Amini Islands, U. T of Lakshadweep 682552.
    ambroseroyson@dcmsme.gov.in
    brdcdi-laks@dcmsme.gov.in

21. EFC, MSME-DI, Rajainagar Industrial Estate,
    West of Chord Road, Poopsite to Fire Station,
    Bangalore 560010. Karnataka.
    sumansraju@nic.in

22. EFC, Branch MSME-DI,
    L-11, Idustrial Area, Yeyyadi,
    Manglore, Karnataka 575008.
    sruthigpoduval@gmail.com

23. EFC, MSME-DI, C Block, CGO Complex,
    Seminary Hills, Nagpur, (Maharashtra)
    Pin 440006.
    msmevijay@gmail.com

24. EFC, MSME-DI,Vikas Sadan,
    College Square, Municipal Colony, Cuttack,
    Odisha 753003.
    dargadc@yahoo.co.in

25. EFC, Branch MSME-DI, C/9,
    Industrial Estate, Rourkela 769012. Odisha
    suvendu.kumar@gov.in

26. EFC, Branch MSME-DI,
    R.K. Nagar, Rayagada 765001. (Odisha)
    nkratnam23@gmail.com

# Enterprise Facilitation Centres (EFC) of MSME-DI

27. EFC, MSME-DI,
    10, Industrial Estate, Polo Ground,
    Indore 452003. MP,
    rk.mohnani.msme@gov.in

28. EFC, Branch MSME-DDI, Udyog Vihar,
    Chorhata, Rewa 486006.
    rk.barnwal.msme@gov.in

29. EFC, MSME-DI, Kurla Andheri Road,
    Sakinaka, Mumbai 400072.
    bsathe.iss@gmail.com

30. EFC, Branch MSME-DI,
    Aurangabad, P-83 Chikalthana, MIDC,
    Naregaon Road,
    Aurangabad 431006.
    subasj468@yahoo.com

31. EFC, Branch MSME-DI,
    Patel Road, Ramnagar,
    Coimbatore, (Tamil Nadu) India 641009.
    kayalvizhi.b@gmail.com

32. EFC, Branch MSME-DI, No-6,
    Jeyaraj Road,Tuticorin,
    Tamil Nadu 682002.
    jerinamsme@gmail.com

33. EFC, MSME-DI, Industrial Area B,
    Ludhiana 141003. (Punjab)
    mkvmsme@gmail.com

34. EFC, MSME-Development Institute, (Govt. of India, M/o MSME),
    22 Godam Industrial Estate, (Opp. Godam No.02),
    Jaipur 302006.
    Ph-0141-4012482,
    Tele Fax-0151-2210553
    bhatnagar.tarun@gov.in

35. EFC, PPDC - Extension Centre, Industrial Area,
    Basni Road Rotary Choraha,
    Nagaur 341001. (Rajasthan)
    goutam.msmetdc@gmail.com

36. EFC, (MSME-DI), Chennai- No. 65/1,
    GST Road, Guindy Industrial Area,
    Chennai 641009. (Tamil Nadu)
    jayachandiran@gmail.com

37. EFC, Branch MSME Development Institute,
    RA39 (Ground Floor), Urvashi (Phse-II),
    Bengal Ambuja, Tarashanar Sarani,
    City Centre, Durgapur 713216. (West Bengal)
    tkbanik2016@gmail.com

38. EFC, MSME - Development Institute,
    R. N. Tagore Road, Suri, Birbhum 731101.
    Phone: 03462 - 255 402.
    sksen.msme@gmail.com

# Enterprise Facilitation Centres (EFC) of MSME-DI

39. EFC,MSME-DI Narsapur Cross Roads,
    Balanagar, Hyderabad,
    Telangana 500037.
    sumathi.msme@gmail.com

40.  EFC, MSME-DI,
     Kham Bungala Campus, Kaladungi Road,
     Haldwani 263139.
     Uttarakhand
     dcdi-haldwani@dcmsme.gov.in,
     pushkar_bisht12@yahoo.in

41.  EFC, MSME-DI, 107, Industrial Estate,
     Fazalganj, Kapali Road,
     Kanpur 208012.
     amit.msmeknp@gmail.com
     mail.9451787939@gmail.com

42.  EFC, Branch, MSME-DI,
     Industrial Estate, Dollygunj, Port Blair 744103.
     Andaman & Nikobar Islands
     amit.msmeknp@gmail.com
     mail.9451787939@gmail.com

43.  EFC, MSME-DI
     A-Wing, 3$^{rd}$ Floor, CGO Complex,
     Sanjay Place, Agra 282002.
     mksharma@msmediagra.gov.in

44.  EFC, MSME-DI, E-17/18,
     Industrial Estate, Naini, Allahabad 211009.
     Uttar Pradesh (Jointly setup by DI & PPDC)
     sps.msme@gmail.com
     rajan.msmetdc@gmail.com

45.  EFC, Br MSME-DI,
     Industrial Estate, chandpur, Varanasi 221106.
     Ph-0542-2370621
     rakesh.chaudhary@dcmsme.gov.in

46.  EFC, MSME-DI.111 &112,
     BT Road, Kolkata 700108.
     sitanathm@dcmsme.gov.in

47. EFC, Branch MSME Development Institute,
    RA39 (Ground Floor), Urvashi (Phse-II),
    Bengal Ambuja, Tarashanar Sarani,
    City Centre, Durgapur, West Bengal,
    Pin 713216. tkbanik2016@gmail.com

# EFC of Technology Centers

1. EFC, MSME-Tool Room
   (Indo German Tool Room)
   Plot-5003, Phase-IV, GIDC Vatva Mehmedabad Road,
   Ahmedabad 382445. (Gujarat)
   vsigtr@gmail.com

2. EFC, MSME-Tool Room (Indo Danish Tool Room)
   M-4 (Part) Phase-VI,
   Tata Kandra Road, Gamharia, Jamshedpur (Jharkhand)
   pswain@idtr.gov.in

3. EFC, MSME-Tool Room (Indo German Tool Room),
   P-31, MIDC, Chikalthana Indl. Area,
   Aurangabad 431006.
   awsekar.gs@igtr-aur.org; gm@igtr-aur.org

4. EFC, MSME-Tool Room
   (Central Tool Room & Training Centre)
   B-36, Chandka Industrial Area,
   P.O. Patia, Bhubaneswar 751024. (Odisha)
   skkar@cttc.gov.in

5. EEC, MSME-Tool Room
   (Indo German Tool Room),
   Plot No. 291/B-302/A, Sector-'E'
   Sanwer Road Industrial Area,
   Indore 452003. (MP)
   vineetgarg1973@yahoo.co.in

6.  EFC, MSME-Technology Development Centre
    (Institute for Design of Electrical Measuring Instruments)
    S.T. Tope Marg Chunabhatti, PO Sion,
    Mumbai 22. training@idemi.org

7.  EFC, MSME-Technology Development Centre
    (Fragrance & Flavour Development Centre),
    GT Road, Industrial Estate ,
    P.O. Makrand Nagar, Kannauj (U.P.)
    bairwababulal@yahoo.com

8.  EFC, MSME-Technology Development Centre
    (Process cum Product Development Centre)
    Sports Goods Complex,
    Delhi Road Meerut 250002. (U.P.)
    vksingh@ppdcmeerut.com

9.  EFC, MSME-Tool Room (Central Tool Room)
    A-5, Focal Point,
    Ludhiana 141010. (Punjab)
    training@ctrludhiana.com

13. EFC, MSME-Technology Development Centre
    (Process cum Product Development Centre) Foundry Nagar,
    Agra 282006. (U.P.)
    ashwin.msme.tdc@gmail. com

10. EFC, MSME-Tool Room (Central Institute of Hand Tools)
    G.T. Road, Bye Pass,
    Jalandhar 144008. (Punjab)
    adtrainingciht@gmail.com

14. EFC, MSME-Technology Development Centre
    (Central Footwear Training Institute)
    C - 41&42, Site 'C' Sikandra,
    Industrial Area, Agra 282007. (U.P.)
    sudhanshusharma855@gmail. com

11. EFC, MSME-Technology Development Centre
    (Central Footwear Training Institute)
    65/1 G.S.T. Road, Guindy,
    Chennai 600032.
    kolanjivel@cftichennai.in

12. EDC, MSME-Tool Room
    (Central Institute of Tool Design)
    A-1 to A-8 APIE,
    Balanagar Hyderabad 500037. (Telangana)
    dy.directortrg@citdindia.org

15. EFC, MSME-Technology Development Centre
    (Centre for the Development of Glass Industry),
    A-1/1, Industrial Area, Jalesar Road,
    P.O. Muiddinpur, Firozabad 283203. (U.P.)
    jpyadav.cdgi2018@gmail.com

16. EFC, MSME-Tool Room
    (Central Tool Room & Training Centre) Bonhooghly Indl.
    Kolkata 700108. (W.B.)
    hk.choudhury@msmetoolroomkolkata.com

# EFC of Technology Centres

17. EFC, MSME-Technology Development Centre
    (Electronics Service & Training Centre),
    Kaniya, Ramnagar,
    Dist. Nainital 244715. Uttarakhand
    pd_estc@estcindia.com

18. EFC, MSME-Tool Room (Tool Room & Training Centre),
    Amingaon Industrial Area, North Guwahati Road,
    Amingaon, Guwahati 781031.
    trtcghy@hotmail.com

# EFC of PPDC, Agra

19. EFC, PPDC - Extension Centre, Jaipur,
    17-18 A, Bais Godam Industrial Estate
    Jaipur 302006.
    deepakmnit175@gmail.com

20. EFC, PPDC - Extension Centre,
    Thiruvalla, C/o MSME Training Institute,
    Manjadi P.O., Changacherry,
    Thiruvalla, Kerala 689105.
    balaguru.msme@gmail.com

21. EFC, PPDC - Extension Centre, Ettumanur,
    C/o MSME Testing Station,
    Industrial Estate, Ettumanur,
    Kerala 686631.

22. EFC, PPDC - Extension Centre,
    Jodhpur, Plot No. A1-A3, Udhyog Bhawan,
    New Power House Road, Industrial Estate,
    Jodhpur 342003.
    deepakmnit175@gmail.com

23. EFC, PPDC, Foundry Nagar,
    Agra 282006. UP,
    rajkumar.msmetdc@gmail.com

24. EDC, MSME DI, Allahabad, E-17/18,
    Industrial Estate, Naini,
    Allahabad 211009. U.P,
    rajan.msmetdc@gmail.com

25. EFC, NITTE School of Management,
    govindapura, Gollahalli,
    Yelahanka, Bengaluru,
    Karnataka 560064.
    vijay.msmetdc@gmail.com

26. EFC, PPDC - Extension Centre,
    Madurai, C/o MSME Skill Training Centre,
    SIDCO Industrial Estate,
    Melur Road, K. Pudur,
    Madurai 625007.
    jayachandiran@gmail.com

27. EFC, PPDC - Extension Centre,
    Kolhapur, C/o MSME Testing Station,
    P - 31, MIDC, Shiroli,
    Industrial Area, Kolhapur
    prateekmsme@gmail.com

28. EFC, PPDC - Extension Centre,
    Kota, Plot No. A1-A2,
    D.C.M. Road, Industrial Estate,
    Kota 324007.
    deepakmnit175@gmail.com

29. EFC, PPDC - Extension Centre,
    Udaipur, Plot No. A1-A2,
    Industrial Estate, Pratap Nagar,
    Udaipur 313003.
    deepakmnit175@gmail.com

30. EFC, Uttar Pradesh State Room No. 15 &18,
    Expo Mart Kaiserbagh Officers Colony,
    Quisarbagh, Lucknow 226001.

31. EFC, Sanskriti University,
    28, K. M. Stone Mathura,
    Chennai - Delhi Hwy,
    Chhata Rural, Uttar Pradesh 281401.
    rajkumar.msmetdc@gmail.com

32.  EFC, PPDC - Extension Centre,
     340/342 Coindia Complex, Avarampalayam Road,
     K. R. Puram, Coimbatore 641006. (Tamil Nadu)
     vijay.msmetdc@gmail.com

33.  EFC, MSME DI, 65/1,G.S.T.
     Road, Guindy, P.B. 3746,
     Chennai 600032. (Tamilnadu)
     jayachandiran@gmail.com

# National Small Industries Corporation
# Office Addresses:

| S. No. | State | Name of the Field Office | Nodal Office |
|---|---|---|---|
| I. | Uttar Pradesh | 1) Agra | **Kanpur** |
| | | 2) Ghaziabad | NSIC Limited |
| | | 3) Noida | 112/1, $2^{nd}$ Floor, Benajhabar Road, |
| | | 4) Kanpur | Kanpur 208002 |
| | | 5) Naini | Tel: 0512-2535049 |
| | | 6) Lucknow | Tele Fax: 0512-2556379 |
| | | | Email: bokan@nsic.co.in |
| | | 7) Varanasi | |
| | | 8) NTSC Aligarh | |
| II. | **Uttarakhand** | 9) Dehradun | **Dehradun** |
| | | | NSIC Limited |
| | | | Near Sabji Mandi,Niranjanpur, Saharanpur Road, Dehradun – 248 001 (Uttranchal) |
| | | | Tel: 0135-6451005 |
| | | | Tele Fax: 0135-2520501 |
| | | | Email: bodehradun@nsic.co.in |
| III. | **Punjab** | 10) Jalandhar | **Ludhiana** |
| | | 11) Ludhiana | NSIC Limited |
| | | | Guru Gobind Singh Tower, G T road Near Dholewal chowk |
| | | 12) NTSC Rajpura | Ludhiana 141 003 (Punjab) |
| | | | Tel: 0161-41946/2546523/ 2530940 |
| | | | Telefax: 0161-2531946 |
| | | | Email: boludh@nsic.co.in |
| IV. | **Haryana** | 13) Bahadurgarh | **Faridabad** |

| S. No. | State | Name of the Field Office | Nodal Office |
|---|---|---|---|
| | | 14) Faridabad | NSIC Limited 107, NISSAN HUT NH-5, Railway Road Faridabad (Haryana) - 121001 Tel: 0129-4311292,4311252 Telefax: 0129-4311293 Email: bofaridabad@nsic.co.in |
| | | 15) Gurgaon | |
| V. | Chandigarh | 16) Chandigarh | Chandigarh NSIC Limited SCO - 378, 2$^{nd}$ Floor, Sector-32, D, Chandigarh Tel: 0172-2620538, 2620539 Fax: 0172-4656538 Email: bochd@nsic.co.in |
| VI. | Delhi | 17) Delhi | Delhi NSIC Limited Branch Office Delhi, NSIC-TSC Okhla Campus, Okhla Ind. Estate, New Delhi-20 Tel: 011-26382567/26382568-69 Fax: 011-26382427 Email: delhinsic@nsic.co.in |
| | | 18) Head Office | |
| | | 19) NTSC Okhla | |
| | | 20) Jahangirpuri | |
| | | 21) Naraina | |
| | | 22) Parliament Street | |
| | | 23) Wazirpur | |
| VII. | Chattisgarh | 24) Raipur | Raipur NSIC Limited 204 – II Floor, Block – A, Crystal Arcade, Near Lodhipara Chowk, Shankar Nagar, Raipur – 492 007 (C.G.) Raipur – 492 007 (Chattisgarh), Tel: 0771-2432915, 0771 – 4035388/6006070, Telefax: 0771-2445490 Email: boraipur@nsic.co.in |

| S. No. | State | Name of the Field Office | Nodal Office |
|---|---|---|---|
| VIII. | Maharashtra | 25) Mumbai | **Mumbai** NSIC Limited Branch Office, I$^{st}$ Floor, Prestige Chambers, Kalyan Street, Majsid (E), Mumbai - 400009, (Maharashtra) Tel: 23740268 23740272 Telefax: 022-23741989 Email: bomum@nsic.co.in |
| | | 26) Andheri | |
| | | 27) Aurangabad | |
| | | 28) Nagpur | |
| | | 29) Pune | |
| | | 30) Nasik | |
| IX. | Rajasthan | 31) Jaipur | **Jaipur** NSIC Limited NF/0/2 Nehru Place, Tonk Road, Jaipur 302015 (Rajasthan) Tel: 0141-2742991/ 2742372/2742944 Fax: 0141-2741277 Email: bojai@nsic.co.in |
| | | 32) VKIA Jaipur | |
| | | 33) Bhiwadi | |
| X. | Gujarat | 34) Ahmedabad | **Ahmedabad** NSIC Limited 202, Samruddhi Building, Near Old Gujarat High Court, Ahemedabad-380 014 Phone: 079-27544893, 27541301 Fax: 079-27540159, E-Mail: boamd@nsic.co.in |
| | | 35) Surat | |
| | | 36) NTSC Rajkot | |
| XI. | Madhya Pradesh | 37) Bhopal | **Bhopal** NSIC Limited 110, Malviya Nagar Bhopal-462003(Madhya Pradesh) Telefax: 0755-2766205, 2553183 Email: bobpl@nsic.co.in |
| | | 38) Indore | |

| S. No. | State | Name of the Field Office | Nodal Office |
|--------|-------|--------------------------|--------------|
| XII. | Andhra Pradesh | 39) Vijayawada | **Vijayawada** |
| | | | NSIC Limited |
| | | | No. 59A-8/8-6B/1, III Floor, Main Road, Gurunanak |
| | | 40) Visakhapatnam | Colony, Vijayawada, Krishna District, Andhra Pradesh–520 008 |
| | | | Tel: 0866-2541055 |
| | | | Tele Fax: 0866-2545055 |
| | | | Email: bovijayawada@nsic.co.in |
| XIII. | Telangana | 41) Hyderabad | **Hyderabad** |
| | | 42) Balanagar | NSIC Limited (South203, Sri Dattasai |
| | | 43) NTSC Hyderabad | Complex, RTC 'X' Road, Musheerabad, Hyderabad-500020 (Andhra |
| | | 44) EMDBP Hyderabad | Pradesh) |
| | | | Tel: 040-27622515/ 27615761/27622097 |
| | | | Fax: 040-27617777 |
| | | | Email: bohyd@nsic.co.in |
| XIV. | Karnataka | 45) Bangalore | **Bangalore** |
| | | | NSIC Limited |
| | | | No. 25, I$^{st}$ Main Road, KSSIDC |
| | | 46) Peenya | Industrial Estate, 6$^{th}$ Block, Rajajinagar, Bengaluru – 560010 |
| | | | Tel: 080-23109059,080- |
| | | 47) Belgaum | 23307791, 080-23147858 |
| | | | Fax: 080-23300070 |
| | | | Email: boban@nsic.co.in |

| S. No. | State | Name of the Field Office | Nodal Office |
|---|---|---|---|
| XV. | Tamilnadu | 48) Chennai + STP Chennai | **Chennai** NSIC Limited Branch Office New No 422(Old No 615), Anna Salai, Chennai – 600006,(Tamilnadu) Tel: 044-28293347/28294541/ 28294066/28292056 Fax: 044-28295791 Email: bochen@nsic.co.in |
|  |  | 49) Ambattur |  |
|  |  | 50) Coimbatore |  |
|  |  | 51) Madurai |  |
|  |  | 52) Trichy |  |
|  |  | 53) NTSC Chennai |  |
| XVI. | West Bengal | 54) Kolkata | **Kolkata** NSIC Limited 20-B, Abdul Hamid Street, (7th Floor) Kolkata – 700069, (West Bengal) Tel. :033-2213-7084/2248-7357/58/0015 Fax: 033-2248-7359, Email: bocal@nsic.co.in |
|  |  | 55) Salt Lake |  |
|  |  | 56) Durgapur |  |
|  |  | 57) New Market |  |
|  |  | 58) NTSC Howrah |  |
| XVII. | Orissa | 59) Bhubaneswar | **Bhubaneswar** NSIC Ltd DIC Campus, Rasulgarh Industrial Estate Bhubaneswar Phone: +91-674-2549780, 2548875 Email: bobhubaneswar@ nsic.co.in |
|  |  | 60) Rourkela |  |

| S. No. | State | Name of the Field Office | Nodal Office |
|---|---|---|---|
| XVIII. | Assam | 61) Guwahati | **Guwahati**<br>NSIC Limited<br>(Branch Office), Industrial Estate, Bye Lane No.3 Bamunimaidam, Guwahati-781021 (Assam)<br>Tel: 0361-2657952, 2657947/48<br>Res. 2730219<br>Fax: 0361-2550981<br>Email: bogwh@nsic.co.in |
| XIX. | Bihar | 62) Patna | **Patna**<br>NSIC Limited<br>104 I$^{st}$ Floor, Manna Surti Complex, Doctors Colony, Kankarbagh Patna 800 020 (Bihar)<br>Tel: 0612-3212403, 0612-2354222<br>Fax: 0612-2354222<br>Email: bopatna@nsic.co.in |
| XX. | Jharkhand | 63) Jamshedpur<br><br>64) Ranchi | **Jamshedpur**<br>NSIC Limited<br>Vikas Bhawan<br>Complex, Adityapur Jamshedpur-831013 (Jharkhand)<br>Tel: 0657-6004051<br>Telefax No. 0657-2371299<br>Email: bojms@nsic.co.in |

| S. No. | State | Name of the Field Office | Nodal Office |
|--------|-------|--------------------------|--------------|
| XXI. | Kerala | 65) Cochin | **Cochin**<br>NSIC Limited<br>Branch Office, S–67 GDCA<br>Complex, Marine Drive<br>Ernakulam, Kochi,<br>Cochin – 682031 (Kerala)<br>Tel: 0484-2381850/2368149*<br>2366288<br>Fax: 0484-2380155<br>Email: bococh@nsic.co.in |
| XXII. | Dadra & Nagar Haveli | 66) Silvassa | **Silvassa**<br>NSIC Ltd.<br>105-106, Hotel Viraj Building,<br>Opposite Gurudev Complex,<br>Sayli Road, Silvassa - 396230.<br>(UT of Dadra & Nagar Haveli)<br>Tel/Fax: 0260-2640272<br>Email: bosilvassa@nsic.co.in |
| XXIII. | Puducherry | 67) Puducherry | **Puducherry**<br>NSIC Limited<br>Administrative Building,<br>Industrial Estate,<br>Thaffanchavady,<br>Puducherry-605009<br>Tel: 0413-2248970,2248940<br>Fax: 0413-2248970/2248940<br>Email: bopon@nsic.co.in |

➤ Nodal Office for the following States shall be:

A) Goa             -   BO Mumbai

B) Himachal Pradesh   -   BO Chandigarh

C) Jammu & Kashmir   -   BO Ludhiana

D) States in North East   -   BO Guwahati